A Book of Cutting

stories of gardens and gardeners in Berkshir

Published by Corridor Press
21 South Street
Reading
Berkshire RG1 4QR
England
Telephone: (0118) 9391029

Printed and bound in Great Britain by
Antony Rowe Ltd, Bumper's Farm, Chippenham, Wiltshire, England

ISBN 1 897715 25 0

Corridor Press publications:
See It! Want It! Have It! (1992)
Bricks & Mortals (1994, reprinted 1994, 1996)
Moments of Glory (1996)
A Book of Cuttings (1997)

Under the imprint Corridor Poets:
The Dark Larder Lesley Saunders
Einstein's Eyes Tim Masters
Scratched Initials Susan Utting
Small Infidelities Kristina Close

Volunteers are welcome to join Corridor Press book projects or attend our courses and workshops on all aspects of writing and publishing. You can contact Alison Haymonds or Linda Maestranzi at Corridor Press, 21 South Street, Reading RG1 4QR, telephone (0118) 9391029.

A Book of Cuttings

stories of gardens and gardeners in Berkshire

Illustrations by ROMILLY SWANN

CORRIDOR PRESS

PREFACE

A Book of Cuttings is a gardening book in which gardeners and the people who love gardens are as important as the gardens themselves. More than 100 volunteers, from schoolchildren to pensioners, have contributed to give a fresh and individual look at gardening in Berkshire, ranging from the great gardens of the past to today's allotments and community gardens, as well as the private passions of local garden lovers. You will find a mixture of stories, memories, and good advice which we hope will entertain, intrigue and inform.

The books produced by Corridor Press provide, we hope, pleasure and information in equal measures to readers and writers alike. Since our aim is to involve people from the whole community in planning, writing and producing our books, the process of making the book is as important as the end product. However we are intent on producing high quality books of which we can all be proud and we hope *A Book of Cuttings* is no exception.

As a non-profit making organisation we rely heavily on the help and friendship of volunteers and supporters. Our thanks, as ever, go to our main funders Southern Arts, Reading Borough Council and Berkshire County Council who are a constant source of encouragement and help in every way.

The Paul Hamlyn Foundation, a staunch supporter of small publishers, provides funding for most of our training courses, and the Reading Evening Post, a paper which believes in supporting community projects, gives invaluable publicity as well as funding.

Through individual grants from The Earley Charity, Slough Borough Council, and Wokingham Borough Council, we have been able to buy essential equipment for producing the book.

Special thanks go to Linda Barlow, the County Arts Officer, who cheerfully transcribed tapes and raised money by selling plants; to Romilly Swann, a brilliant artist, who managed to produce simultaneously the illustrations and a baby; volunteers Nicci Carslake, Gina Bovan and John Davey who helped well beyond the call of duty; Imogen and Damian Clarke, of Imaging Design, who run workshops and give ungrudging help and advice with design and layout; the irreplaceable Dermot and Betty O'Rourke who turn their hands to everything from writing to delivering books; Ron Pearce who took the photos and gave hours of help; Gianna Crolla who gave valuable practical and technical help; Elaine George of LMS Engineering for technical support; the ever-helpful Local Studies section of Reading Central Library; Catherine Olver for arboricultural advice; Ronnie Rutherford for providing illustrations; Steve Ward and Dave Tibbetts, of Reading Borough Council, for information on allotments; and last but not least Torsten Louland for thinking up the title when we had all despaired.

Alison Haymonds and Linda Maestranzi, Project Workers

CONTRIBUTORS

Editorial team:
Elsie Bailey
Rosie Bass
Gina Bovan
Nicola Carslake
John Davey
Rose Davis
Anne-Marie Dodson
Phil Fortune
Alison Haymonds
Elinor Jones
Margaret Kelly
Torsten Louland
Linda Maestranzi
Bunty Nash
Betty O'Rourke
Dermot O'Rourke
Roy Pelling
Romilly Swann
Susan Utting

Contributors:
Chris Baines
Tony Barham
Pat Barlow
Michael Barratt
George Bartlett
Rosie Bass
Lisa Bate
Paul Bavister
Gina Bovan
John Bowsher
Gerald Bradford
Gladys Bradford
Morina Bryan
Prof Stefan Buczacki
Roy Cecil

Sydney Clarke
Alison Coe
Pat Cooper
John Cox
Dorothy Cripps
Hester Davenport
Olivia Davenport
John Davey
Rose Davis
David Downs
Karen Edwards
John Evans
Mike Facherty
Bob Flowerdew
Phil Fortune
Tina Gower
James Gumbs
Ray Harrington-Vail
Alison Haymonds
Joan Head
Felicity Hertslet Kaplan
Margaret Hnatiuk
Len Hurrell
Anne Ibbetsen
Maureen Johnson
Elinor Jones
Margaret Kelly
Ted Kelly
Dr Harry Leonard
Torsten Louland
Duncan Mackay
Linda Maestranzi
Chris Martin
Allan Meakin
Bunty Nash
Diana Nicholas
Betty O'Rourke

Dermot O'Rourke
Lois Parker
Ron Pearce
Roy Pelling
Josephine Perry
Sue Phillips
Sheila M Plank
Harold Poole
Reg Prickett
Ted Prickett
Derek Prout
Bernard Redway
Betty Reed
Reg Rhodes
Ian Richardson
Bessie Ridley
Sheila Rooney
Gordon Rowley
Bob Russell
Lilian Skeels
Margaret Skinner
Joe Simpson
Olive Simpson
Iqbal Singh
Malki Singh
Ray Smith
Peter Swinn
Anne Swithinbank
Marjorie Sykes
William V Tate
Jeremy Taylor
Sheila Tibbles
Charles Tringali
Linda Tringali
Susan Utting
Gerry Westall
Jennie Winter

Pam Woodcock

Schools:
Bearwood Primary
Grazeley Primary
Kennel Lane
Knowl Hill
Park Lane Primary
Ranikhet Primary
St Teresa's RC Primary

Artist:
Romilly Swann

Photographer:
Ron Pearce

Design and layout:
Imogen and Damian
Clarke

Typography/transcription:
Linda Barlow
Gina Bovan
Kirsten Bunch
Nicola Carslake
Gianna Crolla
John Davey
Anne-Marie Dodson

Proofreading
Betty O'Rourke
Dermot O'Rourek
Gina Bovan

Editor
Alison Haymonds

PICK OF THE BUNCH

All these people have helped to make *A Book of Cuttings* possible by buying copies in advance. A donation has also been made to Trunkwell Park teaching and therapeutic centre, Beech Hill.

Rosemary Andrews
Diana Bawdon
Mary Baxter
Alexander Beasley
Matthew Beasley
Mrs J M Bellworthy
Mrs Yvonne Bicknell
J and P Bishop
Mrs Patricia Ann Booden
Mr Philip Bowerman
Mona Bunch
M and M Burridge
Mrs J Butcher
Patricia, Jack, Kate and Ray Callow
Mr Joseph Carey
Nicola Carslake
Jean Clargo
David and Kate Cripps
Dorothy and Bob Cripps
Susie Da Costa
Anne-Marie Dodson
David Downs
Mr and Mrs J Anthony Fish
Rowena Gale
Carrol Gabriel
Mrs Eileen Gilkerson

H W Granger
Barbara, Mike and Chelsea Haddon
Ron Hayward
Norman Hill
Jill and Mike Hollidge
Matthew Hollingworth
David C Maddock
Maria Maestranzi
Mr and Mrs E Maton
Sally Moore
Mrs H Moriaty
Betty and Dermot O'Rourke
Mr Clive Thomas Parsons
Mr D Putt
Norma Renton
Dr Ian Richardson
M J Skinner
Mrs K Speers
Maureen Stallard
Mrs Jo Swinn
Mrs Moira Taylor
Mary and Brian Warwick
Mrs Marion Watters
Mrs Diana Wicks
Miss Rosemary A G Woodman
Mrs M N Wookey

CONTENTS

FOREWORD

A colleague at the University once congratulated me on heading a department so relevant to everybody – "There are landscape and garden designs all around us, and most things in supermarkets not in tins are Horticulture!" he said. A bit exaggerated, perhaps, but I know what he meant – especially in comparison with his own department, Applied Statistics!

Our university subject is a professional one, and so the motivation, management, economics, investment, technology and environmental impact are all very different from "Gardening". It is a pity that professional horticulture and amateur gardening are so often equated in people's minds. Gardening welds production and amenity into a common purpose hardly possible in the professional field. Yet gardening is often the introduction that leads students to study horticulture at university, for there is in common the love of plants, vulnerability to the vagaries of the climate and a supreme and often unwarranted optimism!

It is these characteristics of gardeners, rather than gardening in its own right, which make the collection of personal reflections and goals in *A Book of Cuttings* so very delightful. It is a book to read in sequence rather than to dip into, at least the first time around! This is because the rewards of reading it stem as much from the contrasts between adjacent chapters as the contents of the chapters taken in isolation.

I wish you very much pleasure with this book – which although small, has a big heart. I am sure you will find that the 'cuttings' which comprise the chapters will find, in you, very fertile ground for taking root!

Helmut van Emden
Professor of Horticulture
The University of Reading

To Linda Barlow,
County Arts Officer,
who represents the
best of Berkshire

God Almighty first planted a garden; and,
indeed, it is the purest of human pleasures.
Francis Bacon
Of Gardens

I beseech you forget not to inform yourself as
diligently as may be, in things that belong to
Gardening, for that will serve both yourself and
your friends for an infinite diversion.
John Evelyn to Mr Maddox,
10th January 1657

He who plants a garden, plants happiness.
Chinese proverb

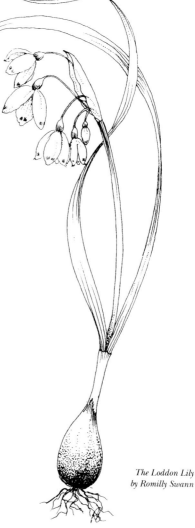

The Loddon Lily
by Romilly Swann

a for abbots walk

The garden in the ruins

The first time we saw the garden was across galvanised fencing which divided our car park from what looked like a sea of mud, covered with huts. The huts formed temporary accommodation and rest-rooms for the builders working on the adjacent office block. At that time we were so delighted with our newly renovated apartment that we hardly gave a thought to what the area would eventually look like, although we were told that in a year or two there would be a sunken garden.

After a couple of years the offices were finished, the huts removed, the earth-moving equipment moved in and, in almost no time at all, the developers, MEPC, had recreated the cloister of Reading Abbey, albeit in horticultural form. I had never really managed to summon any degree of enthusiasm for formal public spaces, but I was both surprised and impressed by the planting of 'our' garden. Commonplace garden shrubs such as roses, lavender, catmint, and mahonia appeared alongside exotic ornamental grasses and bamboo.

I have no idea who designed the garden, but I love the combination of sculptural forms which reflect the rugged character of the ruins, and the summer underplanting of brightly coloured annuals. Substantial timber pergolas were erected on both north and south sides of the garden and in spring these are now covered in wisteria, honeysuckle and clematis. All around the garden are

JENNIE WINTER

In the heart of Reading lies an unusual and beautiful garden which recreates the cloister of Reading Abbey, whose ruins border one side. This is a special place for the people who live in the garden apartments of Abbots Walk, as JENNIE WINTER explains

secluded bowers where office workers come to rest and relax in the middle of the day.

There can be very few gardens in Britain which can claim to be bounded on one side by the remains of a medieval building which once hosted parliamentary sittings, but if there are any ghosts they are benign ones. Most visitors are usually struck by the peaceful nature of the place. However, on a misty autumn evening it was possible to get rather a nasty shock if you weren't aware that the hooded figure striding out across the grassy bank below the refectory wall is actually an Elizabeth Frink bronze sculpture; this has recently been relocated within the garden, thus losing much of its dramatic effect.

In high summer, this area presents a very different picture when the foot of the wall is obscured by a border of dark red, mixed roses. The mixing is in itself a piece of inspired planting for it avoids the appearance of a formal garden bed and gives added interest in the subtle differences of shade and form. The wall itself is covered in an ancient ivy and a lilac tree has rooted in the mortar. This section of the ruins was not included in the major renovation which took place in the early eighties. Work was halted due to lack of funds. Now the wall of the refectory is home for squirrels, mice and small birds.

The garden has become a special place for many regular visitors who value its peace. It is a place to bring very small children who can play safely in the green 'playpen' of the sunken lawn. It is used for outdoor receptions during summer and for rehearsing open air Shakespeare; it forms a backdrop for many wedding pictures and during the last summer became the venue for a Thursday evening croquet competition organised by one of the companies next door. Over the years the garden has acquired trees and shrubs planted to commemorate those who have been associated with it in some way and are now sadly dead, and on a happier note it boasts a crab-apple

> **How vainly men themselves amaze**
> **To win the palm, the oak, or bays,**
> **And their incessant labours see**
> **Crown'd from some single herb or tree,**
> **Whose short and narrow-vergèd shade**
> **Does prudently their toils upbraid;**
> **While all the flowers and trees do close**
> **To weave the garlands of repose!**
> **Andrew Marvell**
> **'Thoughts in a Garden'**

tree planted to celebrate 'Dorian's first birthday'.

There is little doubt that this has quickly become a place which people think of with affection. For our three cats it is their territory. They are the feline guardians of the garden and ensure that any rodent which dares to set foot in it is hastily dispatched. Unfortunately they have also tried to ensure that it remains a silent space by pursuing any bird which strays into it. However, the magpies which inhabit the old yew tree which overhangs the garden ensure that the balance of nature is retained. They terrify the cats!

The cloister garden, sketched by Romilly Swann

Living in close proximity to such a beautiful place, the residents of the garden apartments of Abbots Walk try to compete with it, and with each other, by decorating their small patios in both summer and winter with a variety of floral baskets and pots of all shapes and sizes. The patios face due south and figs and grapes flourish and ripen in such a sheltered spot. The vine which covers the patio of Number 12 gives a distinctly Mediterranean feel to the whole area. When we first came to live at Abbots Walk, I thought that I should miss the large country garden which I had formerly owned. Nothing was further from the truth. I have had far more pleasure from pushing pots around my postage-stamp patio than I ever had from a third of an acre, and I have the added pleasure of sitting in the sun, enjoying my lunch and a glass of wine whilst the gardener mows the lawns and tends the garden just beyond.

We have felt very privileged to live in this place. The ruins of Reading Abbey are a magnificent sight at any time of the year and the sensitive planning of the cloister garden has enhanced the site. I have photographed the 'cloister' under snow and wearing its spring and autumn colours. It is the chosen location for group pictures of our ever-growing family of children and grandchildren and when we leave Abbots Walk, the garden will feature as part of a pictorial record of the most creative decade in our lives.

Those who visit us marvel that such a beautiful and secluded place should be in the very heart of Reading. It has been our very own 'secret' garden which we enjoy sharing with all those who come to appreciate its peace and beauty.

THE LONG WALK

At the turn of the century, my grandparents occupied a house in Orts Road, Reading, one of a number built for employees of Huntley and Palmers biscuit factory. The hours of work were long and arduous, the working day did not finish until 6pm, and 1pm on Saturdays.

In spite of the unrelenting demands of his employment, grandfather kept an allotment. It was by any standards an astonishing distance from his home, situated in Shinfield Road, believed to be somewhere near the Pepper Lane junction. Not only was it almost a two-mile journey on foot but nearly all uphill by way of Watlington Street, Craven Road, Addington Road and Redlands Road. He often took his two youngest children with him, my father and my aunt.

He must have been a most energetic man, insisting on walking at four miles an hour, pushing a small handcart containing garden tools and collecting manure on his way. His vegetables were acclaimed as successful and praiseworthy. They needed to be. A Victorian-sized family on a factory labourer's wage needed careful economy.

Bob Russell

a *for allotments*

Fresh from the garden

Even when Joan Head was a young girl in Berne, Switzerland, she preferred gardening to dolls. She remembers one day when she and her brother were off school, her father gave them jobs to do. "He told my brother to weed the garden path. To me he said: 'You go and do your knitting.' Young girls had to do as they were told in those days. But when he had gone, we switched jobs. I did the weeding and my brother did the knitting. It all started from there."

Now, at 75, Joan is still gardening, resolutely clearing the weeds and digging the drought-hardened soil of her new plot in what is left of the Amersham Road allotments, in Caversham. In February 1997, she had to leave the plot she had nurtured for 13 years to the mercies of the bulldozers which are now clearing the site for 190 new houses.

"I heard the site was being closed down two years ago," she said. "The first thing I knew was when I read in the paper that it was going to be built on. I went mad and I got on the phone to the council. That's three times I have lost my allotment in 30 years."

She mourns the things lost on her old plot: her young oak, grown from seed, her 'noble fir' and the bed of asparagus – 'it was the first year I have been able to pick them'. The only things she brought with her, raspberry canes and strawberries, immediately perished in the dry soil. But she is not deterred. "Really I'm too old to change but I was determined I was going to do it."

Standing in what looks like a building site, weeds knee high

Most days, JOAN HEAD leaves her seven cats at home and pushes her bike to her allotment. She's a well-known character at the Amersham Road allotments, Caversham, where she has had a plot since 1968

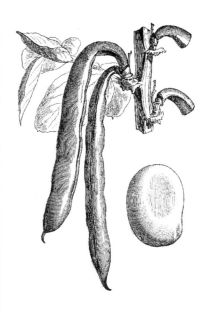

stretching around her, she and a handful of other allotment holders are optimistically starting the long process of creating order out of chaos. She is installed with her shed (already broken into twice), her tools, her bird-box and her cigarettes and already beans are sprouting and peas and carrots are on their way. "Actually once I've cleaned and cleared the ground, the soil is not bad," she said.

Joan came to England when her father, who was living over here with her stepmother, became ill with heart trouble. For a time she worked in Sussex as a housekeeper and gardener, then came to Reading in 1960 with her father and found a job on the buses.

"I had split up from my husband and needed something to do, so I got an allotment at Amersham Road, on 'B' field. The first allotment, 'A' field, was built over, and eventually 'B' field, and 'C' field, where I had my second plot, were taken for housing.

"There were all sorts of allotment holders in those days, older people, families, students who had allotments to learn on. Most have gone now. My first year was spent cleaning up and tidying. In those days the council rotavated the plot for you free of charge but the best thing to do for clearing ground is to grow potatoes; they suppress the weeds. I also grew runner beans, peas, carrots, beetroots, celery, onions. I had some soft fruit as well – I grew everything. I knew how to grow things from seed from watching my father and he had learned from an uncle who owned a farm.

"When I first started my allotment, ten poles cost 12 shillings and 6 pence for a year. After two years, we all had notice to quit and when we reapplied, it had gone up to £3. But after doing all the work and having all the aggro, you had to carry on.

"I moved on to my second site on 'C' field in 1984. But the soil was no good. 'A' field had the best soil, 'B' field the second best, and 'C' was the worst. There was hardly any top soil and it was stony – that's why they kept pigs there. There were pigs all over the site until they fell sick and everything had to be whitewashed inside and out.

'I cook beans the Swiss way. Pick them when they are young, sweat an onion with a bit of garlic in some fat, add the beans, sweat them, then add salt, summer savory, a piece of bacon, a couple of potatoes, tomatoes, a little bit of water, and cook for an hour or 20 minutes in a pressure cooker. Cook peas when they are young. Add the heart of a lettuce, sugar, butter, pearl onions and salt, and cook very very slowly. I also cook carrots in the Swiss way, with a touch of garlic and onion, sugar and salt, a little bit of water, bacon and potatoes. They are always telling you you mustn't eat butter. Rubbish! I eat my butter, and my milk and cheese. You need all that. Fat keeps you warm, your body needs it.'
Joan Head

The purple narrowboats Jemima and 'Cutty' Pedalduck, owned by the Swann family of Reading, are floating gardens. Story on page 33.

Above: Lithops villetii var deboeri

Below: Conophytum frutescens

Succulents painted by Romilly Swann

Above: Gordon Rowley Below: The glasshouse, Cactusville (July 1970). Story on page 39

"The allotment I took over was like a football pitch but I really got cracking and soon turned it over. I had a machine to help clear it but I prefer digging. These machines only cut the roots and spread them about. I really had to work on that piece of ground – stones, stones, stones , bricks, garden things, glass, chamber pots, you name it, I've dug it up. It hasn't changed. I'm still waiting to dig up something interesting.

"Over the years you improve the ground with lots of digging and putting in different elements. I've added all sorts of manure, peat, grit, liquid manure to give plants a boost. Once we got elephant manure when the circus was visiting! Anything grows really well if you tend it. I have my own compost heap and put everything on it but it takes some years to rot down.

"I grow all the vegetables I need and freeze everything. There are a lot of old people round here so I give away any surplus vegetables and fruit. Every year I grow potatoes, beans – which are my favourites – peas, carrots, onions, beetroot. My beans didn't do well last year. We haven't had any rain for the last two winters, just a little dribble. The seasons and the weather are changing, and the vegetables can't tell if it is summer or winter. They need warm nights, and a nice shower in between.

"I love herbs. On my old plot I had a rosemary bush, summer savory, basil, parsley, chives, garlic, a bay tree, thyme, sage, oregano, camomile – that's good for an upset tummy.

"I don't think there is a secret to gardening. It's hard work, but the reward justifies it. I get pleasure out of growing things. It's good to get out of the house. You get exercise, you don't get fat, you are in the fresh air, it is lovely in the sunshine as long as it is not too hot.

"In the old days, there were no freezers or convenience foods which could just be shoved in the microwave. That is not food in my opinion. I like to cook my own meals, fresh from the garden. It's a different vegetable when you grow it yourself."

JOAN HEAD – 'I get pleasure out of growing things"

Digging for Victory

There were many established allotments in and around Newbury before the Second World War and a lot were started even before the First World War but the food situation didn't get as bad as it did in the 1939-45 conflict. The ones I remember best were at the end of Greenham Road and Howard Road where the Newbury ring road is, to the east and south of the town. Most are gone now.

I can remember as a boy going up to the allotments in Long Meadow. There was a lovely little lane wending its way up the back of the workhouse and these old boys would sit there by their little huts, pipes in their mouths, of a summer's evening and those plots would be hoed immaculately with not a vestige of a weed. They grew all their own vegetables. They've all gone now, and I suppose if they were still there it would be a job to find people to bother with them today. We've got quite a lot of vacant allotments in Newbury.

There was a big allotment area at Westfields, down Kennet Road, and the fortunate ones to have plots there were very successful because it was near the river and the soil was really black and rich. At the time of any drought they used to go down to the river with a bucket and some of the more enterprising ones had a hose and would suck it and let it run. There was another big allotment area at the Four Hatches where children used to fish for bream and perch. Allotments were very much sought after by people who didn't have big gardens.

Many of the allotments were expanded considerably for food production during the Second World War – Dig for Victory it was called. I'd been discharged from the army and I got an allotment in Bartlemy Road, near the grammar school, where some of the playing-fields had been taken over for that purpose. We had all types there, men who had been discharged from active service, war workers, the local doctor, accountants.

Allotments were at their peak during the Second World War when parks and fields were turned into productive plots to help the war effort. GERALD BRADFORD remembers the war years in Newbury when co-operation was the keyword for allotment holders

Of course a lot of these allotment keepers were older people and I noticed they often used to put in flowers amongst their vegetables, particularly ones which produced a scent – obviously for cross-pollination. In many flower gardens, vegetables like lettuces and beetroot were added to the colour schemes.

Because of the shortages, things had to be invented. They say necessity's the mother of invention. I remember people used to make cold frames with old bricks and wood and a piece of window glass over them. One of the problems of wartime gardening was the shortage of certain seeds. Onions were particularly scarce in those days. I remember men used to plant their onion seed one at a time, two or three inches apart.

We used to pool our resources. A lot of garden clubs and allotment clubs were set up, and when the seeds were in short supply someone would undertake to grow brassica for the group, and someone else would grow a certain cabbage, or a type of lettuce. People were all friendly then and gave each other advice. I hadn't done much gardening with vegetables at that time, and I learned a lot from these men who'd been doing it for perhaps 30 or 40 years. This co-operation was a great thing. We co-operated in every way, and co-operation ultimately brings victory, as we all know .

Now those allotments have gone back to playing-fields. The need is not so great and we have the choice of vegetables from all over the world now. But I can't say the vegetables and fruits are any better than those grown in the natural climate of this country.

HACKED HARD EARTH

Hacked hard earth with a pickaxe
then piled manure planted beans
deep in soil that crumbled
came alive with weeds pulled away
from the food that grew
new seeds for next year –

dug soft earth with a spade
then piled manure planted carrots
deep in soil that breathed
came alive with insects rubbed
from the leaves that fed
new roots for next year –

forked soft earth then raked
away weeds planted onions
shallow in soil that steamed
came alive with morning dew
that filled out bulbs piled up
in the shed for next year.

Paul Bavister

Tilling the soil in urban areas

Our site comprises 36 allotments. It is bounded on one side by a lane of mature houses and on the other side by a row of 28 houses built in the 1950s.

You will notice that I refer to 'our site', because that is how we feel about it. Seven plots are cultivated by on-site residents, who can just pop out of their back doors to cut a lettuce, to add a bucketful to their compost heap or to lean on a spade to have a gardener's gossip. Most of the rest of us live nearby and are made to feel very welcome and part of the club. Peter, who lives on site, has a hot line to the borough recreation department and does a wonderful job as our link on general maintenance matters.

Now comes the really fascinating part, where everyone does his or her own thing – TOOL SHEDS. A few are of standard design – prefabricated with one window and a strongly locked door – very trim and prim. Others show great ingenuity in the use of recycled timber, windows and doors. They often do double duty as greenhouses. One or two are so luxurious that they resemble the classic Russian-style 'dachas', where it is not unheard of to settle down for a drink and a snooze after a bout of digging! We at the minimalist end of the scale store our tools horizontally in what is known as 'Bunty's Box'.

When it comes to cultivation there are several distinct styles. First there are the proud possessors of mechanical rotavators – large, noisy beasts that rush up and down and chew up everything in sight, but somehow don't get rid of the the perennial weeds. Then there are the serious double diggers, who often have as well a treble spit deep trench ready for that delicious compost to encourage next year's runner beans.

Both these methods lead on naturally in the Spring to immaculate, perfectly parallel rows for seed sowing and cultivation. I have to admit that I have never succeeded in planting two perfectly

BUNTY NASH

BUNTY NASH has had an allotment in Reading for many years. She believes the sense of community the allotments engender as well as the satisfaction of growing your own produce are a vital part of urban life. Could there not be less architectural grass and more allotments and play areas between the streets? she asks

parallel rows of anything. On our plots (ours being Ken's and mine) things are quite chaotic. Ken likes straight lines, so he takes care of the framework for the raspberries and tayberries. He served in Burma during the war – that, as you may readily surmise, makes us septuagenarians! He is an expert after his jungle experience in tying poles together so that they don't blow over. Whilst he is occupied one end, I am busy putting my own theories into practice at the other end. I am definitely a non-digger; partly because digging bores me and partly owing to our recent dry summers. I find that I get better results with masses of top-dressing. I have trained some of our friends, who still possess lawn-mowers that actually collect the grass, to leave bags of mowings on our doorstep. We also have a lively compost heap augmented by Jill and Pete's contributions from their tame rabbits and guinea-pigs.

I make a feeble attempt at a few rows of seeds in the Spring, taking only that piece of advice about 'sowing thinly'. Long ago I decided to sow only when the soil was damp and I felt in my bones that Spring was around the corner. I had realised that all those dates recommended on packets were also being read by crofters in the Orkneys five or six hundred miles to the north. Then I do very little thinning. In dry weather, the stronger seedlings of the root crops grow down to the moisture and just shoulder aside the weaker seedlings, so they are not disturbed by ritual thinning – at least that's my theory and I'm sticking to it!

My favourite area is my wild-flower garden. There everything is allowed to seed and that means masses of multicoloured cornflowers, often with goldfinches

BULMERSHE

Insects dragged soft bodies
up stems on allotments steaming
with a winter's wet.
Between creaking sheds I shook
warm dirt on rows of seeds –
a flint with a hole bounced
up from the sieve. I stared through
to cotton fluff caught in reeds
and the two-toed print of a bull
slowly filling with a spade's rust.
Blue flames whispered names from the reeds.
I dropped the flint.

Plastic bottles knocked on sticks.
Pigeons above the roaring road
clapped to a stop in oak scrub.
I wrapped the last leeks in a bin liner
cut string to thread the flint
above the shed door. Cold stone
rubbed clean. Dust blown from the hole.
The shriek of a hawk
being chased by crows
to the old oak.

Paul Bavister

balanced on the seed heads, and ancient red carnations that actually have a perfume. There are wild flowers like yarrow, mallow and poppies between the flowering shrubs and when the sun shines the patch is alive with butterflies and bumble-bees.

To conclude our story, we are just welcoming Maureen and her guide dog Millie to a vacant plot. Fortunately September is an ideal time for starting. I only wish that local authority accounting systems could manage this more often. Maureen has chosen a half-size plot near the water tank and a strong post where Millie can be secured whilst she is working. Owing to her very limited sight, Maureen has decided that her only tool has to be a trowel. She aims to plant as many scented flowers as possible. We have already had many offers of help with clearing the plot, and it will be an ideal time for her to plant the shrubs she has been promised.

I think finally that this little story has reinforced my belief that small allotment sites serving adjacent housing work well. Perhaps town planners could economise on large areas of what I call 'architectural grass' and give opportunities in more secure, sheltered areas between streets for allotments and children's play areas.

LEEKS AND HOLES

Once the milder weather draws near, it is time to plant the season's vegetable plot. One veg I've grown for years, with some success, is the leek. Now, I'm not talking about your 3in diameter show specimen, rather something slimmer, but with excellent flavour. I attribute some of the success to the way in which I form the hole into which the young seedling is placed. My practice has been to make it with a plant-pot corer. This removes a cylindrical, or slightly conical, plug of soil instead of compressing the soil as inevitably happens when using a dibber. I gently place a 9in (approximate) seedling in each hole and flood with water each day – unless it rains – until the seedlings are established, and standing erect. The quality of the mature leek owes something, I believe, to the improved drainage of the non-compacted hole.

Roy Cecil, Datchet

Getting your hands dirty

My first visit to an allotment was on doctor's orders rather than as an answer to economic problems. I needed more exercise and the thought of fresh vegetables as an extra to keeping fit, sounded better than the boredom of traditional methods like jogging, or swimming. My fellow allotment holders were only too willing to aid my efforts in reforming the waist-high weeds into a well-manicured garden of Eden. This, I discovered, was purely based on selfish reasons, as there is nothing worse than an unattended plot, blowing nature's bounty of wild seeds across your crops.

Carrots and Brussels sprouts were the first fruits of my labour. Dutifully I placed them on the kitchen table like the great male provider, ready for my little lady to fulfil her part. My wife would not participate in the role-play. There was a problem to overcome, fighting the elements as well as every slug within a forty-five yard radius. I had considered, but my wife was unaware, that mud is the natural packaging of most vegetables and not the cellophane wrapper of our local supermarket. It took the first taste to convert her to the benefits.

The Cherry Orchard, in Stoke Road, with 250 plots, is the biggest allotment in Slough. Here on these modern plots, with brick-built lock-ups and paved paths, you are more likely to see turbans bent over the weeding, and young mums digging, than the traditional cloth cap and beer belly normally associated with this scene. Sexism and racism lag way behind the important issues, like who can grow the biggest onion, or the longest carrot. Here, I thought, would be a good place to discover what benefits other people actually get from allotments.

Morina Bryan was originally from Anguilla, the most northerly of the Leeward Islands in the West Indies. High on her list of priorities is taste. Redundancy left Morina with time on her hands, so growing

A couple of years ago, Toby Jessel, the Conservative MP, decided he had found an answer to long-term unemployment – an allotment. His rallying cry was 'taking up an allotment would be a positive step which could be a healthy activity and at the same time relieve poverty'. PHIL FORTUNE discovers what allotment holders on the biggest site in Slough have to say

vegetables seemed an ideal way to pass the day and help with the family budget. No chemicals are used on her plot and as Morina says, "It's better eating than the shops. Take runner beans; they may look nice on the shelf but they taste of nothing."

A sense of achievement also features high on Morina's list. When I asked if any family members helped with the digging, Morina explained, "I have two sons both willing to help but if I dig it myself then I know I did it. The pleasure is in getting it done yourself."

Iqbal Singh who is now retired, also does all the digging himself. When I spoke to him, he had only had an allotment for four months, but is no stranger to the land as he had his own farm in India. "It's a bit smaller than our farm," he joked. "I like to come at the weekend just for a look and a walk around."

"Do you grow anything traditionally Indian?" I asked.

"I grow spinach, marrow, onion, garlic, leeks and many other things that I cannot explain in the English language, but no herbs."

I was curious at this, expecting some climatic reason for the lack of exotic herbs, but the reason was far less dramatic.

"I have no experience with herbs," Iqbal said sadly.

A stroll around the other allotments would soon sort out this problem, I thought. There was no shortage of experts here, and more answers than in any book.

Malki Singh, who was busy harvesting what looked like chickweed, was the only person growing something completely new to me. Methi is a Indian vegetable used for curries, as a flavouring in chapattis, or cooked like spinach. Potatoes, onions and garlic all kept Malki's household happy and Malki considered the digging to be good exercise.

When I asked Marjorie Sykes, a mature

The huge Cherry Orchard allotment site in Slough is bursting with productivity

student studying at Langley College, what was her main reason for having a plot, the answer was fired back without hesitation: "Enjoyment, it's the enjoyment of getting away from the family, and doing something I want to do, and that's getting my hands dirty."

Marjorie has a theory about her vegetables. "They don't take as long to cook. Supermarket carrots can take up to twenty minutes to cook, but those from here – two minutes and they're done, and the taste is totally different."

Like everyone else at the Cherry Orchard, James Gumbs was busy preparing his plot for the winter. James managed to combine his shift

Allotment holders enjoy the fresh produce, exercise, the relaxation and the help with their food bills

work with growing West Indian food; pumpkins, corn and peas were his main crop. Pumpkins that can grow up to forty-five pounds are not just used for Hallowe'en lamps, but are the main ingredient in stews and pies. The corn, I noticed, was enclosed with more net than the centre court at Wimbledon. This was the only protection from its hungry enemies.

Len Hurrell, who has the same problem, explained. "Pheasants – they breed in here, and unless you pay close attention to your nets, they will eat the lot.

"They're not the biggest pest though," Len continued. "It's vandals. They get into your lockers and steal your tools; they even took the rotavators off the back of a truck once.

"It's not the same now as when I was young. I used to help my father dig his plot when I was eight years old – that was fifty-nine years ago now. We kept ducks, chickens and rabbits then on our allotment."

Len explained the benefits of crop rotation which meant he had a continuous supply of leeks, cabbage and a new variety of Japanese onion that he was particularly enthusiastic about. "These onions can be used from March onwards as a salad onion, just like a spring onion, or if you leave them they will grow into a big onion."

I asked Len if he ever grew any of his vegetables to show. "No, just to eat," he replied with a look that said, why would anybody want to see them? "I freeze most of it. Take my raspberries. I grow enough of them to last from one season to the next, and that's all for £2.25p a year for this plot and a lock-up. I even manage to grow wallflowers to plant out at home. My plants are grown from seed and I have a greenhouse in the back garden. It all helps keep the cost down."

However, when asked what his main reason was for having an allotment, I was surprised by the answer. "I retired twelve years ago, and this keeps me away from the wife!"

Everyone had their own reason for having a plot on the Cherry Orchard. Morina even waited six months for the privilege. Most people considered the taste of home-grown vegetables and knowing exactly what goes in or on your food the biggest advantages over shop-bought produce. Exercise is a main factor too. Digging a plot in the fresh air certainly beats an aerobics class, and they have company as well. Most gardeners are sociable types, with a preference for leaning on a spade rather than digging with it.

The chance to get away from it all, which is so important to Len and Marjorie, makes it an important form of relaxation. Work or family pressures are easily forgotten once you have nature's problems to worry about.

But the thing that everyone agreed on was that growing vegetables is definitely a major contribution to the family budget. With the rise in popularity of organic vegetables and the constant worries about what we eat, maybe it's not just the unemployed who should be encouraged to take up an allotment but all of us who are looking for a positive step to a healthier life.

Marjorie Sykes, a mature student, explained why flowers are intermingled with her neat rows of vegetables. "I have only got a small garden so I like to grow flowers here; that's how my father taught me to do it."

b *for bearwood school*

Close encounters of a horticultural kind

Jenny Johnson: Last year, in the summer term, Bearwood Primary School had a plant competition and the whole of the school joined in. Mrs Sally Rowe, a parent of a child at the school, supplied everyone with a plant. The children took the plants home for about six weeks and looked after them. We were doing this competition for the environment of the school and to make the school look nice.

When I took my plant home I talked to it every day unless I forgot. My plant grew about twelve flowers. In a while my plant started to droop.

Ruth Millington: My plant just started to droop to one side. I talked to it every day except when I forgot. I called it Maisy.

Todd Nash: My plant didn't grow any flowers and it was lopsided.

Jenny: After six weeks were up, we took the plants back to school and Mrs Rowe judged the tallest plant in each class.

Ruth: Lauren Hunt, Danny Bevins, Alan Bulcock, Esther Gardiner and Andrew Millington, my brother, won for their classes in the junior; I wished I was one of the winners. They won lovely wild-flower books and some about trees.

Todd: When everyone had brought their plants back, the local paper took a photograph of everyone with their plant and published it.

Jenny: Afterwards we planted our plants in tubs around the school. You can still see the flowers which are nice and colourful.
This has been our gardening extravaganza.

Children from BEARWOOD PRIMARY SCHOOL, in Sindlesham, became more closely acquainted with growing things when the whole school took part in a competition which not only taught children how to care for plants but also helped to improve the school environment

b *for beech hill*

The walled garden

When Mr Henry Lannoy Hunter, of Beech Hill House, "a good old English gentleman", died on September 12, 1909, sadly outliving all his three sons, the obituary in the Reading Mercury noted: "The grave was lined with ivy leaves, studded with the white Japanese anemone. At the head lay a beautiful cross of white chrysanthemums and dahlias, the work of Mr F B Thompson, the gardener."

This gardener, Francis Butler Thompson, was the first of three generations of the Thompson family to work in the gardens of Beech Hill House, between 1888 and 1948, and when Mr Hunter's widow died years later, Francis's son, George, in his turn lovingly and skilfully decorated the grave.

George's daughter Dorothy Cripps recalls: "I well remember when old Mrs Hunter died my father lined her grave with roses. He used hairpins to fix these little pink roses from the garden. It seems like yesterday."

Dorothy still lives just across the road from Beech Hill House, at Home Farm, and can see the changes that have taken place over the years to the grand old house and its grounds. In particular she mourns the passing of the superb walled garden, stretching for an acre, which after years of neglect is now being built upon.

Dorothy, who was born in 1927, actually lived within the walls of that garden. When she was 12 she moved into the gardener's cottage

Beech Hill House, in Beech Hill, near Reading, was once part of the manor of Stratfieldsaye, owned by the Duke of Wellington. It was bought by the Hunter family in 1740, and the family continued to live there until the Second World War, when the only surviving daughter, Miss Mary Hunter, gave it to the Red Cross as a wartime convalescent home. In 1955, the Red Cross rented it to a charity, the Ockenden Venture, which looked after refugee children, and it continued as a home until 1968, when it was sold by the Red Cross to boost funds. It is now divided into apartments. DOROTHY CRIPPS, whose family has long links with the Hunters of Beech Hill House, remembers the glories of its garden in the old days with her parents. "The cottage was part of the walled garden," she explains. "We stepped out right on to the outside wall. Two bedrooms, the front room, and part of the kitchen were the actual wall of the garden."

But the house and garden had been part of the family's life long before then. "My grandfather had been gardener for the Hunters for 25 years, when they gave him a lovely roll-topped desk, and when he'd been with them for 60 years they gave him a little Georgian cream jug," said Dorothy. "I think he was more than a gardener to them in the end. I know my dad was.

"My father didn't become a gardener straight away but worked first for a firm that did undertaking and carpentry. It was when my grandfather's sight got bad that my father became the gardener (and gamekeeper as well) and we changed houses. Miss Hunter had a stable block converted for my grandparents to live in, and then our family moved into the cottage in the walled garden."

Dorothy also worked for a year in the garden and her memories of the years when three generations of the Thompsons worked for the Hunter family at Beech Hill House bring back visions of an 'Upstairs, Downstairs' kind of world, where the gardener was summoned by the cook to the kitchen to order the vegetables and the greenhouses were heated by coal fires.

Francis Thompson was still a young man in 1888 when he started at Beech Hill. "My grandfather had been working as an under-gardener at the Lockinge Estate in Ardington," said Dorothy. "In those days people used to recommend their gardener to other big houses if they were looking for somebody. It was quite a feather in his cap to become head gardener at Beech Hill. I don't know what he earned when he started but his wages in 1944 were £5 for two weeks. Because he helped look after the woodland, he earned another 10 shillings. He had two men under him to help him with all those box hedges, flower beds and lawns as well as the walled garden."

Dorothy Cripps as she is now and (below) in 1942 when she was 15

Dorothy remembers the garden so well she can still draw detailed plans from memory. "In front of the house was a circular lawn with plants in the middle and all the way round. The lawn used to be cut by a horse-drawn mower and the horse had special shoes made of leather fitted over its shoes so it didn't make a mark on the lawn.

"There were heated and cold greenhouses and a conservatory in which orchids were grown. My one regret is that when they sold the conservatory and the bits and pieces from the garden before Beech Hill House itself was sold, I didn't try and get one of those orchid pots. I would have appreciated it more now than at the time."

But it was the walled garden that really caught Dorothy's imagination. "It had its own vinery for grapes, but the actual roots stretched outside. I believe, in years gone by, if a horse died on the estate, its carcase was put in the ground there to provide blood and bonemeal for the grapes to live on."

The garden was filled with an abundance of fruit and vegetables: "It had all these lovely espaliered fruit trees and the fruit was fantastic. Right the way round the inside of the wall there were plum, peach and pear trees and on the outside wall there were morello cherries, dark red, and covered with nets against the birds. I used to poke my fingers through the nets to pinch one. I remember the fig trees, which carried this year's fruit and next year's fruit at the same time: you can see the tiny fruits which take a year to ripen. There was so much of everything that when all the best fruit had been taken, mother used to make wine from the fruits that weren't good enough or had been rained on and had gone squashy. She also made raspberry vinegar for coughs in the winter.

"There was a Worcester apple tree, Cox's Orange Pippins and Blenheims, and Russets around the back. The fruit was stored on racks

Dorothy's grandfather Francis Thompson (above right) and her father George (above left) standing against one of the splendid espaliered trees. (Below) The scene in summer 1997 in the walled garden looking towards what was the stable block as the site was being developed for building

in the apple store, and I remember it smelled horribly of rotten apples and a rat would look at you! The apples used to keep very well in those days, as long as you were careful how you picked them.

"I don't think they ever had to buy any vegetables, maybe some special exotic things. There were enough fresh vegetables going for the whole house, celery and leeks and artichokes and asparagus. I remember they put salt on the asparagus beds to keep the weeds down – it was beautiful asparagus, really fat pieces. These days a lot of it's all spindly. There were nice early lettuces, which had been overwintered, and artichokes, which are not grown much now. Some of the artichokes around now have a sort of head on them, and you bring out the taste of the petals with butter, but these artichokes you dug out and they were like knobbly potatoes, with rather a smoky taste, and they would make artichoke soup out of them.

"Carrots and potatoes were stored in heaps of sand. Nothing was wasted – even the peapods were made into soup. And there was kohl rabi, like a big turnip with knobs on, which I remember being grown by the wall. And after the best quality vegetables had gone to the house, we had what was left over.

"They used to have a big water-tank, and if anybody had a sheep, they used to collect the sheep droppings in a sack and then put it into the water-tank. I can remember that quite well – going round the farms to pick the stuff up – a cheap way of getting liquid manure!"

During the Second World War, Dorothy's father asked permission from Miss Hunter to buy a horse to plough up the village cricket-field for agricultural use. This was to keep the field in the Hunter family

"The Hunters had their own little milking herd which also had to be looked after by the gardener. Cream and butter was made in a proper little dairy where we had to churn out and make butter and set the big pans on a marble table for the cream to rise."
Dorothy Cripps

The garden at Beech Hill House in its heyday

rather than have it commandeered by the Government. They also took on another field to grow corn. This horse like the others was kept in the old stable beyond the walled garden: "It had glazed blue tiles all around it – it was a beautiful stable," said Dorothy.

It became Dorothy's turn to work in the garden when she was 14 years old. Help was hard to come by with many men away in the forces, but she would much rather have been a nurse.

"I was engaged for the sum of 14 shillings a week, but I only stayed for a year because Miss Hunter couldn't afford to keep me on. I was lucky because that was when the British Red Cross were taking over Beech Hill House, and that gave me my first taste of nursing.

"I just accepted I had to work in the garden – you did in those days. Some jobs I didn't like. I hated picking some of the fruit – gooseberries, blackberries, black- and red-currants if it was hot, but it was lovely when the peaches were ripening because if there was a fallen peach, it would be mine! I enjoyed it when the boxes of Sutton's seeds came, which had been ordered from a catalogue."

Miss Hunter was by now the only surviving member of the family at Beech Hill and she handed over the house to the Red Cross although she continued to live in part of it. Many young children came to stay there, some of whom had been treated badly and were crawling with lice or had other health problems, and Dorothy went to help nurse them. Much of the gardening work was curtailed, although the conservatories were kept up, but when the house was passed on to the charity Ockenden Venture, the walled garden began to be run down.

"They did bits and pieces which we could see out of our cottage window, but they didn't make a very good job of it," said Dorothy. "Eventually it was allowed to go to rack and ruin. It's very sad when you remember what it used to be like."

"In the heyday of the garden, we had cold frames near the cottage and there were parma violets planted in them – they were beautiful, and the perfume from them! As Sunday-school children we used to pick them for Mother's Day. Even the leaves had this gorgeous perfume. I'll never forget the perfume of the ivy-leaved geraniums, and the size of the heliotropes in the conservatory. They grew to about 12 feet tall, trained up wires, and their perfume would go right into the sitting room."
Dorothy Cripps

Miss Hunter (in Red Cross uniform), the only surviving member of the Hunter family, pictured in 1945 with the children who stayed at Beech Hill

Left: The garden of the house in Eldon Square, Reading, where Felicity Hertslet Kaplan and her family lived. Story on page 57.

Below left: The scented memorial garden at Folly Court, Wokingham, owned by the Guide Dogs for the Blind Association. Story on page 59.

Below right: Herbalist Lilian Skeels amongst the foliage in her Bracknell garden. Story on page 81.

George Bartlett's fascinating fuchsias. Above: Winston Churchill;
right (top) Stanley Cash, (bottom) Flirtation Waltz. Story on page 62.

b *for boat gardens*

Floating flower borders

Some may wonder if, considering the limitations, it is worth the effort of maintaining a garden on a boat. The 'Thames to Kennet' based Swann family, who live aboard purple narrowboats Jemima and 'Cutty' Pedalduck, have to say emphatically yes.

Upon the roofs of these boats flourishes a necessarily low but surprisingly vital garden. Such a garden is admittedly quite labour-intensive but provides ample reward of fresh fruit, vegetables and herbs through the year to a veritable feast of vibrant colours and scents for all.

The season begins in the artist's studio on the Cutty in which early each spring every available space is crammed with seed trays. Most seeds have been collected the previous year from old colour-co-ordinated favourites such as purple petunias, violas, campanulas and pansies, plus for contrast fiery-hued nasturtiums, marigolds and mesembryanthemums. The other seed trays contain vegetables, including tomatoes, zucchini, cucumbers and lettuces, and herbs like parsley, chives, coriander and sage.

Outside, bulbs, polyanthus and winter pansies are flowering amongst Swiss chard and radishes. The spring sap is rising after the cold winter lull and the most admired rhubarb is creaking to life in its tub under the tiller, promising many more delicious crumbles.

As the season progresses, the seedlings are planted out in pots, tubs and troughs amongst the established perennials and fast-

Everyone who knows the Thames and the Kennet, knows the Swann family with their two 'water babies'. Artist, mother and sailor ROMILLY SWANN does not let life afloat stop her from cultivating her garden

emerging beloved anemones. With a little cosseting it is not long before the garden again is resplendent, luxuriant and spangled with blooms.

During the summer months, care must be taken to water consistently, as everything dries out easily. Of course there is no excuse for neglect in this matter as water should never be in short supply. (My husband might add that, when watering, should you fall in, don't take the plants with you, as neither they nor wife forgive too easily.)

The plants are fed very sparingly as any excess ends in the river, which probably already contains enough fertilizers to account for the incredible vitality of the boat garden.

Regular dead-heading helps keep plants flowering and some need pruning to keep them short enough to clear low bridges. One year however a foolishly sanctioned red sunflower shot up to four foot above the roof, only to be cruelly decapitated by the number 231 bridge on the Oxford canal.

The only other lofty individual is a recently acquired family apple tree, up which a purple clematis climbs. Much pruning will be needed, but hopefully they will bear fruit of each type.

The riotous colours of summer never fail to attract attention and the boats are often photographed, painted and filmed, most notably in the latest 'Inspector Morse' film in which the garden had a passing moment of glory.

Whenever we travel the waterways, people are very generous with cuttings and seeds, plus choice blooms for painting. It is gratifying to

Vicia sativa
14.5.94

be able to return such kindnesses.

Many beautiful private gardens adorn the banks of the Berkshire rivers, especially the Thames. Irresistible stripy lawns hold back burgeoning herbaceous borders, humming with cottage classics and exotic treats. Sadly, not all garden owners welcome boat-dwelling enthusiasts but many who do so are as charming as their gardens. Other horticultural havens can only be admired from across the water.

The only other gardens accessible to boats are the odd secluded public garden, such as Chocolate Island on the Kennet backwater in Reading. Lock gardens, of which there are many on the Thames, boast numerous choice specimens worth appraising, for example the clematis at Blake's Lock and heavenly scented honeysuckle, jasmine and roses at Sonning, not forgetting many more upstream and down at the seventeen other Berkshire locks.

The thirty-five locks on the Kennet don't have kept gardens as such, but many pretty wild flowers and garden escapees garland lock gates and watersides. One striking alien is the Indian balsam which is rampantly invading Britain's waterways. The secret of its success and fascination is the explosive method of seed dispersal. Just touch a ripe pod!

Other extraordinary plants live submerged in water with filigreed leaves or pads like yellow brandy bottles and white water lilies which sink their baldness-curing roots into the rich river mud.

In fact our boats are just a transient flower border in an ever-present water garden.

'CAPABILITY' BROWN

Hannah More tells us that Capability Brown illustrated everything he said about gardening by some literary or grammatical allusion; and he compared his art to literary composition. "Now, there," said he, pointing with his finger, "I make a comma; and there," pointing to another spot, "where a more decided turn is proper, I make a colon; at another part, where an interruption is desirable to break the view – a parenthesis – now a full stop; and then I begin another subject."

A Century of Anecdote (from 1760 to 1860)
John Timbs

b *for burfield lodge*

A gentleman's residence

During the eighteenth century, many fine gentlemen's residences were built in Old Windsor. A couple of these estates remain intact: The Priory, where in the mid-eighteenth century Richard Bateman created a Gothick fantasy house and garden, and Woodside, where Elton John has today established his own fantasy world, including a tram and a life-sized dinosaur. Others, like Burfield Lodge, are gone.

Burfield was built in 1796 in classical style and acquired a reputation for its gardens. There was an Italian garden with statuary, ornamental pools, a rose garden and a walled vegetable garden with a prize asparagus bed, orchards, lawns and an elegant drive lined by slender conifers. Ted Prickett, now in his nineties, remembers how just before the First World War he got his first job there:

Ted: "There's a job going at Burfield Lodge. Go and get it!" – in them days, if you could count to ten on your fingers and you was thirteen years of age and had a job, you could leave school. Anyway, I went and got this job and was sweeping the gardens and leading donkeys with a mowing-machine. Of course, one morning I thought to myself, "I've got a donkey, I'll ride it", so I jumped on its back to take it down to the shed to get the mowing-machine. But the other gardeners done a naughty thing – they poked a broom handle just under his tail. He didn't like it at all! Took me all round the ground, and there was yew hedges all round and he stuck his head down and

Housing estates and a school now cover most of the site where Burfield Lodge once stood in Old Windsor, the village where Elton John has created his own fantastic garden. HESTER DAVENPORT talks to two villagers who still remember the house and gardens as they were

there's where he left me. He went "Hee haw" – "And hee haw to you," I said.

Ted didn't stay long in this job, but in 1930 Bessie Ridley's husband Bill, a skilled gardener, began forty-four years of work there.

BESSIE RIDLEY

Bessie: My husband used to say you were so busy working you never had time to appreciate it, but it was a lovely place with lots of unusual trees and shrubs. There was a beautiful cedar tree, so well looked after that the branches were right to the ground, and when they mowed they had to be very careful to lift them up and mow under so as not to break any. There were five fishponds in different parts of the gardens, and lots of statues – what happened to them all? Seats were cut into recesses of hedges and then you looked down the path and there'd be a statue at the end. One was a pretty Mercury.

The Italian garden was looped for roses, and everywhere there were clipped trees, lots of small 'mushroom' trees and the driveway had twenty-two trees like skittles on either side. Clipping had to start in November and went on till February. One year a picture at Chelsea Flower Show showed my husband clipping one of the yews – to advertise some long clippers. But they were too long, you couldn't clip a mushroom tree successfully with them, so my husband had clipped it first with ordinary shears! They said you could clip as fast with them as ten men, so Bill tried it on the hedges and you'd have had to clip awfully fast to do what ten men might.

In front of the house there were three beds and they were filled with different flowers according to the season. The old vegetable garden had a raised bed at the back and all the rest was one mass of flowers. The old asparagus bed was there that was a hundred years old – beautiful asparagus, that was left there when they moved the vegetable garden, with

The drive flanked with clipped trees 'like skittles'

the flower beds around. After June you don't cut it and you have the feathery foliage which builds up to next year's crop. The new vegetable garden was made out of one of the meadows, and it had two beautiful cherry trees – I think one's left now.

In the war three bombs fell on Burfield – two in the orchards left craters, and one fell by the ornamental bridge and smashed the bridge. A tree at the side took part of the blast and the cedar must have taken the rest, but it wasn't damaged.

During the war my husband had to scythe the lawns as obviously you were only allowed so much petrol, so they only mowed the drive to keep that nice.

After the war my husband tried to keep things going. When the Lodge was sold, people came just to see the gardens. They didn't bother to go into the house. Some land had already gone for housing and then Bill was on his own – he tried to keep the gardens up but it was too much for one person. In summer, he'd work until dark and I used to help him weeding and thinning. I wouldn't have seen much of him if I hadn't.

It was a beautiful garden – but I don't like seeing it now.

Most of what were once the gardens of Burfield Lodge now lie under houses and a school, but the mansion remains, divided into units, as does part of the drive with the trees, their slender forms grown portly with age.

The gardens at the side of Burfield Lodge

C *for cactus*

A touch of the desert

It all began in the early 1930s when my mother, looking for a novel present, spent 6d (2.5p) in the Harrow Woolworth's on a small potted cactus for me. It was a hook-spined *Mammillaria*, and when some weeks later I found a dead fly among the spines I assumed that it was one of those insect-eating plants I had heard about. It didn't respond to my diet of meat and soon expired, but not before I, too, was hooked – on a pursuit that became a lifelong obsession.

After a wartime interruption my growing collection overflowed from windowsills to a small glasshouse, and on moving to a home of my own in Reading in 1967 I set about creating 'Cactusville' with a 7m (24ft) glasshouse divided into three sections: cold, cool and warm, to suit the needs of different types.

By then I had discovered that cacti are just one of several botanical families of plants (succulents) with fleshy leaves or stems that store water and tide them over long periods of drought. There are thousands of them, not to mention oddball variants, and new hybrids that you can make yourself. Searching them out, and acquiring plants, cuttings or seeds, becomes a never-ending challenge and source of fun. Some are tree-like and require bonsai treatment unless your greenhouses are as big as those at Kew. Others are compact or even minute, and these appeal more to addicts, especially those cacti that flower annually. But even when not in bloom they excite admiration for their strange geometrical patterns

Cactus lover GORDON ROWLEY reminisces over his attempts to recreate the desert in his garden in Earley, Reading

and subtle blends of colouring, suggesting surrealist paintings or sculptures in jade.

After years of seeing succulents only in pots or cramped in beds under glass, in 1968 I finally went to see them in the wild: first in south-west USA and Mexico, home of the cacti, agaves and echeverias. Three years later I did a tour of the other great centre of diversity, South Africa, to find tree aloes and euphorbias, stapelias and crassulas, and tiny mesembryanthema hiding in rock crevices, under shrubs, or buried in the soil like stones. In places the whole landscape is filled with succulents so diverse that a whole morning could pass scouring an area no bigger than my garden back at home. Other trips followed and gave a whole new perspective to my understanding of their way of life.

Cultivating succulents comes down to following a few straightforward rules learnt from observing them in habitat. They are creatures of the sun, pre-adapted by millennia of natural selection to survive tropical heat and periodic desiccation. Put in the shade, as on a mantelpiece, they languish and die. They are not fussy about soil as long as it is porous and never remains waterlogged. They need air and food (minerals) just like any other plant, and water to fill up the 'tank', so the popular myth of succulents thriving on neglect in pure sand is just that. Greatest satisfaction comes from raising them from seed, which is not too difficult for many – indeed, you may end up struggling to find homes for all the progeny. Others are next to impossible, and remain as rarities, highly priced when obtainable at all: in other words, the perfect setting for connoisseurs and those who persevere. And how little we still know about their individual whims and idiosyncrasies! But when your very own seedling comes into bloom for the first time, it is worth all the effort spent in raising it.

As inhabitants of warmer climes, very few succulents are adapted to withstand frost. A glasshouse or at least a heated frame is an early

CACTUS SOCIETIES

One of the many rewards in specialising in a minority group of plants, be they succulents, orchids, carnivores or ferns, is the contact it brings you with fellow enthusiasts. There are clubs and societies, books and journals, if you know where to find them.
Beginners are catered for: indeed, societies could not exist without new converts coming in all the time.
There is no better (or cheaper) way to start a collection than via personal contact.
The British Cactus and Succulent Society has more than 3,000 members and branches all over the country. The Reading Branch meets on the third Saturday of each month (except July and August) at 7.30pm in Chapel Hall, Loddon Bridge Road, Woodley, and welcomes newcomers.
Just drop in or ring (0118) 944 1954 for details.

need. However, since schooldays I had the urge to experiment with succulents (surplus or blemished specimens, mostly) outdoors in sheltered sunspots and surrounded by rocks and grit to avoid lying on wet soil. Very few survive a hard winter in the south of England, but the effect can be enhanced by putting out pans or troughs of succulents during the summer months only, and by working in other hardy plants that by their spiky or exotic appearance blend well and add shelter: the fearsome *Araucaria* (monkey puzzle), palms (*Trachycarpus* and *Chamaerops*), shrubby yuccas and *Colletia*, and herbaceous *Acanthus* and *Eryngium*. The result is a rather unusual 'mock desert' that certainly looks different and costs nothing to heat in winter.

So why should anyone want to spend time, toil and money amassing denizens of the tropics, largely inedible, and hardly a good investment for future resale? For many, the aesthetic pleasure of having them around is sufficient justification, with the greenhouse a place of silent retreat away from the daily stress and striving. Some groom them for shows, and take pride in filling a shelf with trophies for the spouse to polish. For the botanist and evolutionist succulents are an endless source of wonder, bristling with unsolved riddles and opportunities for research.

And now conservation is uppermost in the minds of many collectors. Succulents are extremely vulnerable, as many are confined to small areas and could easily be wiped out by the bulldozers or over-eager collectors. Documented collections of correctly labelled specimens are thus becoming increasingly important, and the owners can take pride in propagating and distributing the rarities to ensure their survival.

Who knows? – some may manufacture a life-saving drug yet to be detected, or contain the genes to enable cereals to grow in deserts!

*Marlothistella uniondalensis
painted by Romilly Swann*

C for caversham court

A fine and public place

From the peaceful old garden of Caversham Court beneath St Peter's Church and on the banks of the Thames, you can watch the pleasure boats plying up and down, swans gliding over to Caversham Bridge to be fed, and even, on occasions, rock festival revellers taking a break, oblivious to your presence. But there's a lot more than a view to admire behind the massive old flint wall that shelters Caversham Court from the heavy traffic on St Peter's Hill.

The buildings which remain are largely the 17th century stables and a low-beamed barn which Reading Borough Council now uses as an environmental centre. The allotments contain a model garden maintained by Berkshire Organic Gardeners, a small orchard being planted with local old varieties of apple (and pear) including the famous Blenheim Orange, dye plants, the giant vegetable cardoon, and even a fig tree which has survived from the days of its former glory in the garden of the second grandest house in Caversham.

The original building was erected by Augustinian canons as a Rectory but with the Reformation, in 1538, it was sold to the first of a series of wealthy families who each modified house and gardens to their own tastes. During the Civil War it was owned by Royalists, the Browne family, and bullets from this time are said to have marked their fine staircase. After the Restoration of King Charles II, the Old Rectory, as it was known for several centuries, was leased to a goldsmith from London called Thomas Loveday, and his family was

If you took a vote in Reading for the most beautiful spot in the borough, writes ELINOR JONES, you might well find that the winner was Caversham Court. The main house has gone but the remaining buildings and the gardens are as practical as they are picturesque

to occupy it from 1665 to 1799. It was they who built the quaint brick gazebo which you can still find down on the riverbank, although a thicket of brambles is threatening to engulf it despite the efforts of a local trust. The lower floor was actually a boathouse, and the top floor had windows looking out on three sides over the river valley.

There is also a history of haunting: a carpenter called Pullen who had lived there long before and apparently committed suicide left a chilly atmosphere behind. Other putative hauntees noted 'the rustle of a silk dress and a shadow passing quickly by', while workers currently using the building speak of a 'caretaker' figure being around.

Caversham Court gardens with St Peter's Church in the background

The Simonds family took over the house in 1800 and did not disturb the black mulberry tree on the left as you enter the grounds, or the lime trees, gazebo or yew hedge (whose cuttings are now collected to make a cancer-fighting drug). But they decided to demolish most of the 'striped house' as it was known, and create a bigger, grander one. To this end, a brilliant young architect, Augustus Pugin, was employed. He had designed parts of the Houses of Parliament and Big Ben, and an elaborate mansion arose in the grounds, although the west wing and stable block remained.

The planting too was expanded This was a time of exciting new botanical discoveries in the new worlds which were opening up throughout Victoria's reign, and some fine specimen trees such as the wellingtonia, deodar (native to the Himalayas), cedar of Lebanon and magnolia were planted, most of which have now grown to maturity. There were extensive glasshouses, including a palm house 45 ft long, and fan-trained figs, peaches and other exotic fruits which were trained along the south-facing 'crinkle-crankle' walls, named for their scalloped shape, which still remain below the church, giving an eerie feeling of a place left behind by time.

It's fun to picture it as it was 200 years ago, with peacocks strutting on the lawns, their shrill cries reverberating through Caversham. They even perched on the wall of the old smithy opposite The Griffin, then a thatched country inn, now well known for its folk evenings.

In 1909, Major Henry Caversham Simonds auctioned off his home and it was then renamed Caversham Court. It passed to Lady Moseley, but not for long; bit by bit the buildings were demolished, culminating in 1933 when the council was planning to build a road over it. Plus ça change!

However, it remains as a pleasure garden open to the public with seasonal planting schemes and many recent additional trees, such as the huge arbutus (strawberry tree) whose flowers appear side by side with the scarlet fruit, which are also spangling the ground beneath as I write in December – this was planted as recently as 1981 by the Caversham Ladies Club. You can find a blue cedar now next to the huge copper beech, which has a fantastic carpet of *Anemone blanda* spread underneath in early spring. The '1,000 year-old' yew beyond is certainly 700 years old and the lower branches have collapsed on to the ground and sprouted into a circle of new trees around their parent.

Looking away from the river at this point you can find a medlar, cherry and greengage and, on the riverbank, ornamental pear, plum cherry, sweet chestnut and a wild service tree, a native species normally found only in ancient woodlands.

In the centre of the lawns, next to a black walnut, are two yin and yang-shaped beds known as the red and white beds, designed by Anne Britton, who was gardener for Caversham Court and Forbury Gardens in the 1980s. The white bed contains white forms of

Caversham Court environmental centre plays host to many excellent gardening courses, meetings of wildlife groups such as the Reading Bat Group, conservation groups like BeC (Berkshire Conservation Volunteers), CROW (Conserve Reading on Wednesdays), and Friends of Prospect Park/Waterloo Meadows/Clayfield Copse and other local nature reserves.
Family events like Green Day and the Apple Fayre have become increasingly popular and successful. Many students volunteer to spend some time at the Centre to gain work experience.
For details of courses and other activities or conservation groups based at Caversham Court, telephone (0118) 946 1638.

hellebores, potentilla, variegated grasses, chrysanthemum, fragrant phlox, dianthus and achillea 'Moonshine' as well as artemesia 'Silver Queen'. The red contains flowers, pink rather than red, such as *Bergenia cordifolia* 'Evening Glow', anemone 'Bressingham Glow', astilbe, aster 'Crimson Brocade', penstemons, monarda 'Cambridge Scarlet', incarvillea, sedum, saxifrage and dicentra (bleeding heart).

A border of shrub roses was planted in the 1980s to the left of the steps near the mulberry, including the 200 year-old varieties 'Maiden's Blush' and 'Old Blush' with a heavenly scent when they flower in midsummer. Around this time the then head gardener Trevor Wilton also created the waterfall and pond which is full of interest at all times of year, even containing the rare local wildflower, Loddon Lily; and the raised rhododendron and azalea beds which are splendid throughout the spring.

The herb garden, edged with box, looks as though it could have been here for hundreds of years with its sundial. But this also dates from Trevor's era with its aromatic rosemary, camomile, three sages, lavender and lemon balm to scent your walk.

In 1992, English Nature gave a grant to establish a wildlife garden for community use, especially for schools without one of their own. Hundreds of native plants were introduced including dog rose, blackthorn, blackberry, crack willow, alder, silver birch, crab apple, ivy, honeysuckle, dogwood and many wildflowers. These provide food and shelter for a plethora of birds, butterflies and other animals. It also looks splendid, especially in its autumn colours and laden with crimson hips and berries, down on the riverbank next to the gazebo and many memorial trees and seats presented by grateful visitors testify to the peace and beauty to be found here.

The lawns slope down to the river

THIS HAPPY PLACE

Nor does this happy place onely dispence
Such various Pleasures to the Sence;
Here Health it self does live,
That Salt of Life, which does to all a relish give,
Its standing Pleasure, and Intrinsick Wealth,
The Bodies Virtue, and the Souls good Fortune
Health.
The Tree of Life, when it in Eden stood,
Did its immortal Head to Heaven rear;
It lasted a tall Cedar till the Flood;
Now a small thorny Shrub it does appear;
Nor will it thrive too every where:
It alwayes here is freshest seen;
'Tis only here an Ever-green.

Abraham Cowley
The Garden

C for cenotaph

Where the poppy blooms

Behind the imposing façade of the keep of Brock Barracks in Oxford Road, one of the busiest routes through Reading, lies a quiet, secluded garden, which comes to life and bursts into colour not once, but twice every year.

The colours which bring it to life are not those of flowers and shrubs, because the essence of the garden is its simplicity and austerity. They belong to the medals of the old comrades of the Royal Berkshire Regiment, and to the scarlet and gold tunics of the band of the Second (Volunteer) Battalion of the Royal Gloucestershire, Berkshire and Wiltshire Regiment.

The veterans gather together in July for the annual regimental reunion, and in November for the Remembrance Day service. The garden in which they parade contains the Regimental Cenotaph, dedicated to Royal Berkshiremen who died in two world wars. One of the most imposing monuments in any park or garden in the county, the Cenotaph was designed by Sir Edwin Lutyens, R A, and closely follows, though in smaller proportions, the pattern of the national Cenotaph in Whitehall.

The cost of the building – £3,000 – was raised by past and present members of the regiment, and by the people of Berkshire. It was unveiled in September 1921, with the Archdeacon of Berkshire, the Revd F J C Gillmor, conducting the service of dedication.

Originally the Cenotaph stood in the centre of a simple grassed

Twice a year, the Cenotaph Garden at Brock Barracks in Reading comes into bloom. DAVID DOWNS writes about a garden which has a very special significance

area. However an addition was made to the surroundings in March 1928. The ground around the base was returfed and gravelled paths added. Young trees, *Cupressus macrocarpa*, were planted on three sides. Sutton & Sons of Reading presented the turf and trees, and provided the supervising labour.

The Cenotaph was rededicated after World War Two and a new inscription unveiled by General Sir Miles Dempsey, Colonel of the Regiment, in July 1947. To the Roll of Honour which contained the names of 6,728 Royal Berkshiremen killed in the Great War, was added a second Roll which commemorated the 1,067 members of the Regiment who made the supreme sacrifice between 1939 and 1945. Both Rolls of Honour can now be found in Saint George's Church, within a quarter of a mile of Brock Barracks.

Once the Cenotaph Garden was a focal point for recruits to the Regiment, but Brock Barracks ended its role as a training depot in 1959, when the Royal Berkshires amalgamated with the Wiltshire Regiment to form the Duke of Edinburgh's Royal Regiment. The absence of a regular battalion, together with the need for increased security, mean that now it is rarely seen by the public.

The garden has been walled on three sides and the gravelled paths have become overgrown. The surrounding area has now returned to a lawn trimmed with military precision where the only visitors are birds and the occasional grey squirrel. The backdrop has also altered, with the roofs of the recently-built houses in Brock Gardens appearing between the Cenotaph and the skyline. On the opposite side of the lawn, a row of elm trees screens the Cenotaph from the former parade ground.

The only flowers in the garden are the artificial poppy wreaths placed on the Cenotaph by the veterans in memory of their fallen comrades. The numbers attending diminish each year, but the significance of the garden, which blossoms each July and November, remains constant.

The Cenotaph (sketched by David Downs) is carved from Portland stone, and stands just over six metres high. It was built by local labour, and the King's and Regimental Colours, each hung with a gold laurel wreath, are sculptured on the west and east sides respectively

C *for compost*

The rotter of East Berkshire

Some time in the mid-70s, before the term organic became really fashionable, I came across a book by Lawrence D Hills entitled *Grow Your Own Fruit and Vegetables*. I had recently moved to Datchet, into a house with a garden large enough to spare a few square metres for vegetables, and the book spurred me on to develop a vegetable plot and to Grow My Own. Amongst other things, Hills introduced me to the compost heap and since that time I – or rather my garden – have never been without one.

Although commercial compost bins are readily available – and I don't doubt they work – I have never made use of one. I'm too cost-conscious for that. I prefer instead to knock one together from odd bits of old fence posts, fencing or palettes to form the four corners and sides. If you make two side by side, you need six corner posts and enough timber for seven sides – one side being shared.

A compost heap is, in many ways, like a fire. Both need air and fuel, and both are hottest at the centre. Unlike a fire, the compost heap also likes moisture. The compost heap must be provided with air from underneath – a few old bricks or large stones, laid on the ground at the bottom, allows air to enter – and through the sides. The timber forming the sides can be spaced so as to leave a centimetre or so between each piece but you do not have to be a master carpenter to make it!

The fuel is, of course, the vegetable material which is going to rot

Do you grow your own vegetables? Do you want to save money? Do you have a square metre or two of garden you can spare, where nothing much grows? Do you have a compost heap? If the answers to those questions are yes, yes, yes and no, then now may be the time to be positive about the last, writes ROY CECIL

down. The heap likes weeds, plant remains, vegetable waste, lawn clippings, kitchen waste and soft prunings. A layer of ash from a recent wood bonfire is a useful addition. You can also add the occasional layer of manure or proprietary compost-making material which helps the rotting process, particularly in colder weather.

The heap does not like holly, ivy, lawn moss, man-made fibres, paper or any inorganic materials. Avoid meat waste as well as it attracts rats. Some people add dead leaves but I prefer to keep them separate to produce leaf mould which has a different role.

In order to expose the contents of the heap to the highest temperature, from time to time it needs to be turned, outer contents to inside. This also helps the flow of air. Think again of the bonfire. If you allow spent fuel – ash – to build up, it can extinguish the fire by starving it of oxygen. In very dry weather an occasional sprinkling with the hose will be appreciated.

Now let's look at what is going on inside the compost heap. In an active heap, a complex and violent process of change is taking place. Sure the process can pong a bit but a properly looked-after heap has a healthy rural ripeness rather than being putrid. Billions of micro-organisms work their way through the vegetable matter converting it into compost. In turn larger creatures, insects and worms, feed on the smaller organisms and their wriggling and writhing helps to homogenize the compost.

Gradually as the fuel runs out the heap cools down and is ready for use. Well-made compost provides both nutrient and 'body' for the soil. The humus contains minerals – calcium, nitrogen, potassium, phosphorus – which are essential for plant growth. Gums and colloidal material improve the soil structure, which in turn aids cultivation and promotes air and water movement within the soil.

The compost can be worked into the soil lightly or spread on top as a moisture – conserving mulch. No amount of compost can be too much and the soil texture will improve year after year.

COMMON SENSE

One of the best pieces of advice I was ever given was 'don't believe you can't do something until you try it for yourself'. Just think of all the times people don't attempt to root a cutting because they don't think it's 'the right time', when very often it would take anyway. Or all the people who don't grow a plant they fancy because they've read it is difficult – a lot of times I've grown things wonderfully well until some bright spark tells me it is difficult, whereupon it smartly dies on me.

Sue Phillips

Picking up fallen fruit from around trees and leaves from rose bushes will help lessen the chances of disease re-infecting the parent plant.

Break up old polystyrene plant trays and packaging to provide drainage for containers – it's lighter and cleaner than broken clay pot crocks.

Always plant container-grown clematis with the top of the rootball at least six inches below soil level.

C *for cox green*

The famous flower show

The flower show which has been held every year since 1977 at Cox Green Community Centre is a revival, on a smaller scale, of an event that began at the turn of the century. Popular though it still is, it is modest compared to the original Cox Green flower show which, in its heyday, attracted the attention of the national press, and was patronised by local landowners like Lady Astor, who would sweep in from Cliveden, enjoy a funfair ride and donate prizes so lavish that the children who received them still remember them.

The first show was held on August 27, 1908, and was a horticultural show which covered the villages of Boyn Hill, Cox Green, White Waltham and Shottesbrook. It replaced a smaller show which had been held previously in Cox Green, and the aim was to encourage local professional and amateur horticulturalists to exhibit produce, while combining it with a rural fête. It was held at Ockwells Manor, home of the local landowner, Sir Edward Barry, who, perhaps wisely, was away when the first show took place.

It was a great success. There were races for children and adults, and afternoon and evening concerts by the Maidenhead Town Band. Evening dancing and a funfair kept the locals amused, but pride of place was kept for the exhibitions of flowers, fruit and vegetables. Much of the organisation fell to Mr Bedford, who continued as secretary from 1908 until the show was discontinued in 1940.

By 1912, the show had moved to the grounds of beautiful Kimbers

A flower show has been held in Cox Green, near Maidenhead, for many years since the turn of the century. It has had a chequered history. Famous between the wars, it lapsed for a time through lack of money but is now as popular as ever

House in Cox Green, owned by the blotting-paper magnate Mr Ford, who became the show's president. It continued there until 1933 when Mr and Mrs Ford requested that it be moved to a nearby field.

During that time, the show was run with only one interruption. In 1914, only two weeks before the event was to take place, it was cancelled because war was declared against Germany. In fact it seemed that wartime might kill off the show, but the government's promotion of homegrown foodstuffs proved to be a good impetus. It was held again the following year, and throughout the war all profits went to help the war effort. In 1918, the show caught the eye of the national press, when the Daily Mirror published a photograph of 'the khaki baby' who won the section for children of serving soldiers.

Lady Astor often presented prizes to the baby-show winners during the 1920s and 30s when the flower show flourished; in fact it was so popular that the committee had to ask for extra buses to transport all the visitors.

The outbreak of the Second World War caused more problems and the planned 1940 show was abandoned. During the war years a small show was held at the Victory Hall, in Cox Green Lane – aptly named the Victory Garden Show – which raised money for the Red Cross, but the main flower show was not revived again until 1952, this time on a smaller scale and at a different venue, in a field on Harvest Hill. The show continued successfully into the 1960s (with the original secretary's daughter, Eve Bedford, following in father's footsteps) but interest declined amongst younger people, and when the cost of running the event was greater than the combined donations and entry fees, it seemed that the show really was finished.

But gardeners never give up and Cox Green flower show bloomed again in 1977, since when, despite the absence of funfairs, concert bands and aristocracy, it has proved as popular as ever.

In 1937, the show also had its own 'Lobby Lud' when an Evening Gazette mystery man attended, awarding a prize of a guinea to the person who recognised him.

Kimbers House, Cox Green

51

d *for drought*

Turning off the garden tap

Drought means less biodiversity, fewer flowers, insects and animals. The low water-level in rivers and streams – some of the latter completely dry – has devastated wild life. We need to reduce water extraction by 80 per cent yet commercial firms, golf and racecourses and the unthinking public still water their lawns!

Demand for water has increased over the last 30 years and in some parts doubled. A sprinkler uses 1,020 litres per hour, more than a family of four would use in one day. We all need to think carefully about watering in the garden –'Using water wisely' to quote from the Thames Water advice leaflet. Do we use water wisely?

Plants to choose

Grow drought-resistant plants such as grey-leaved ones, many of which are Mediterranean plants, provided that there is good winter drainage. A good list can be found in Beth Chatto's catalogue of ornamental plants for hot dry conditions and dry shade. Many spring bulbs will do well as will some of the summer flowering ones. Make more use of native plants. Many vegetables are drought-resistant such as brassicas, beetroots, carrots, parsnips, swedes, turnips and the onion family including leeks, Welsh and Egyptian onions and chives.

Mulching

Creating an artificial mulch (dust tilth) with a Dutch hoe has

Dust bowl conditions, tinder dry undergrowth and cracked earth – this is England in May 1997. The Department of Meteorology records at the University of Reading for 1997 show that rainfall in March was about one-quarter of the normal amount. What can gardeners do to help? Sensible planning and practice can cut out the need for wasteful watering says MARGARET SKINNER who cultivates a 'waterless' garden in Caversham

always worked on humus rich soil. Scientists are now recommending leaving the soil to crack. On a large scale, this causes horrific soil erosion once the rains come so I think years of gardening experience wins.

As soon as the soil is warm and damp enough, then other mulches can be applied. Black polythene can be used for strawberry and potato crops. Bury the edges of the polythene in the soil and plant through cross-shaped slits. Make sure that the ground has plenty of humus in it first. There may be an increase in slug population so encourage frogs, toads, newts, beetles, birds and hedgehogs into the garden. This can be achieved with a small pond, piles of leaves, wood and stones and bird boxes. Feed the soil before mulching.

A mulch is made by covering the soil completely with bulky organic matter. Straw, home-made compost, well-rotted manure, bark, even wet newspaper covered with grass mowings or stones and pebbles will reduce moisture evaporation and should save the need for watering at all. Leaves from comfrey plants can be used as a mulch between lettuce. Slugs will go for these rather than the lettuce.

Manure and compost mulches are excellent for supplying nutrients to soft fruits, shrubs, roses and vegetables but be prepared for weeds. Your compost heap may not be hot enough to kill weed seeds. Mushroom compost, spread two to three inches deep, will not contain weed seeds but does have a certain amount of chalk in it so keep it away from lime hating plants.

Save leaves and make your own leaf mould. This is ideal for woodland gardens.

Old carpet is very useful as a mulch and for paths in the vegetable garden. Polythene covering large areas should be spiked with a fork to aid drainage.

Cocoa-shell mulches are useful in the ornamental garden. The shells repel slugs and snails and add plant foods, nitrogen, potash, manganese and magnesium. Cocoa shell has a pH of 5.1 so is on the

The lack of rain in the fields means that fertiliser has been lying inactive and wasted. In past times, good farming practice avoided this because there was more humus in the soil. The better microclimate formed by smaller fields surrounded by hedges, shelter from wind and sun, and a higher water-table all helped. Worldwide the old systems of water harvesting need to be brought back into use to prevent further desertification

acid side of neutral pH 7. At least two inches is needed. Coconut fibre can also be used three inches deep and bark if it has been partially composted. All these materials are expensive.

Composted wood and paper is now available directly from the manufacturers and Municipal Compost is available from some local authorities. Better still is to make your own, which is cheaper and more environmentally friendly (M E Bruce's book on compost-making will help).

Spring is the usual time to apply mulches but now that we are having such dry springs, it would seem better to think of permanent organic mulches, started in the warmer end of autumn. This system reduces the amount of feeding needed. The mulch can always be moved aside to feed specific plants or foliar feed applied.

Sowing seeds

Try deeper V-shaped drills which will give some shelter to the emerging seedlings. Water well before sowing. Sow thinly and cover with dry soil. It is better to sow thinly in succession to avoid the need for transplanting. Self-sown seedlings make strong root systems and survive drought usually without the need for water. Learn from this and sow hardy annuals in the autumn or early spring for colour throughout the summer and thus avoid the need to plant bedding.

Use soil-based composts in tubs and hanging baskets mixing in water-absorbing crystals before planting. These reduce the need for watering by up to four times. Choose the right plants for the site you have and water well before planting.

Shelter from drying winds can be created by using trellis, fine-meshed net or larger shrubs. In the vegetable garden, fleece is excellent over crops especially carrots, creating a microclimate and keeping away carrot fly. Chicken-wire cloches covered with straw will give enough shade to get plants established. Using deep beds and growing plants closer together also saves water. Sunflowers can be

PUDDLING IN
When bedding out plants in dry seasons try 'puddling in' each plant – that is firming in after watering to a mud-pie consistency, then covering with dry soil or mulch

HARDENING OFF
Plants are vulnerable to hot sun and wind and should only be planted when they can withstand full sunlight. The leaves should be toughened for at least a week if the plants come from a greenhouse or shaded area. So move them daily gradually increasing their time in the sun. These plants may need watering every day.

WATERING BEFORE PLANTING
Submerge plant in its pot in a bucket of water until no more bubbles rise. Remove the pot from the bucket and let it drain for several minutes.

used to shade beans. Grow white flowered varieties of beans which
are self-pollinating.

Watering

Never water your lawn in drought, despite advice given by Thames
Water. Once the rains come, lawns always recover. Cut lightly and
leave the mowings on the lawn to act as a mulch. Longer grass
collects more dew. Top-dress in the autumn with coarse sand and
sieved compost. Another fine mulch in the spring after scarifying the
lawn helps it to stay healthy and green. Water should only be used for
newly-planted trees, shrubs, fruit bushes and conifers which also
need to be protected from wind. All these require attention for two
years. Perennials should survive with one year's care but all will do
better if planted in the autumn.

Summer bedding planted while still young before flowering will
do better than pot-bound flowering plants.

Dry areas under trees, near walls and hedges will need extra
attention and mulching.

Runner beans, celery, early potatoes, lettuce and New Zealand
spinach need water to survive. Compost, wet newspaper and comfrey
in the bean trench reduce watering needs. Outdoor tomatoes, once
established and the fruit set, and given a rich mulch, will have a
better flavour without watering.

Try dwarf French beans instead of runner beans. Avoid celery and
use perpetual spinach and Swiss chard well mulched. Plant in a
shallow depression and water individually in the evening or early
morning to reduce evaporation. Avoid evening watering in the
greenhouse when the weather is cold. Sinking flowerpots next to
marrows, tomatoes and beans and directing the water into these saves
wetting the topsoil. Water spreads out underground in an ellipse and
the roots will go down rather than up where they could otherwise
become scorched.

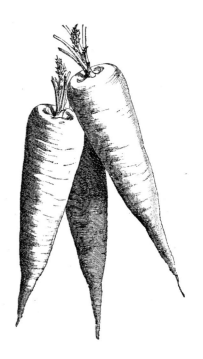

Container gardening is water intensive but stones laid on the top of the pots will keep them cool and damp by reducing evaporation.

In greenhouses use capillary matting or wet newspaper in boxes lined with polythene in spring and summer. This saves time and water. Adding water-holding granules to the compost again reduces the amount of water needed.

Save water by using water butts. These can be joined together. One good shower on a large greenhouse will fill a water butt. After a long drought allow the first shower to wash the dirt, dust and any pollution off the roof, then direct the downpipe into the water butt.

In this area rainwater is better for plants because of the lime content of the local tap water. A tank inside the house, provided that it kept clean, is better still as the water will be at the right temperature for more delicate plants.

Adverts in gardening magazines encourage the use of perforated hosepipe round the garden. This can save time but is potentially wasteful as it waters non selectively .

Grey water, that is water used in the house, can be saved and used in moderation. Better still if it can be run through a reed bed to clean it and make it safer for wildlife. However, not all this water should be used as the water companies need some water to flush out the system.

Much can be saved with a little thought. Boiled water is ideal for watering seeds and cuttings so save any left in the kettle or hot water bottles. Better still, boil only what you need or use a thermos to save water for your next hot drink.

Wash salads and vegetables in a bowl. Weigh up the pros and cons of a dishwasher, bath or shower. Do new houses need to have lawns laid and watered? Why not leave it to the new owners to decide and to see what is really in their garden.

DESIGN FOR GARDENING

It could be argued that the best day for gardening is when the ground is too hard to take a spade, the snow is falling and you're confined to the house with a broken leg. In such seemingly unhappy circumstances, your gardening tools consist simply of pencil and paper – in some senses the most valuable tools you possess, because a garden that's a joy to behold and at the same time to cultivate is the product of thoughtful design in the first place. A few hours' intelligent consideration of all the factors involved can save years of practical frustration.

Michael Barratt
Michael Barratt's Complete
Gardening Guide

e for eldon square

The garden at number 23

Imagine a cold foggy day in November 1968 and an anxious couple driving from London to Reading to view maybe the hundredth house. They arrive in Eldon Square and with much apprehension seek number 23. It's squashed right in the corner and she says, "Looks a bit too small, doesn't it?" They open a gate set between high pillars and walk across a short path of uneven flagstones, surrounded by bushes and climbing plants. They mount fairly steep steps and anxiously wait outside a heavy wooden door.

The house is magical – a central staircase is surrounded by generous room after generous room. The basement is a mess – a small kitchen surrounded by awkward cupboards, leaving a bleak dining room. She knocks down all the walls and visualises one gorgeous open space. The couple peer out of windows, but are confronted by grey fog.

As they reach the end of the viewing, there's a ring at the front door – it's the next lot of people to view. For a few seconds they're alone and say to each other, "It's just right, let's offer the asking price." Number 23 Eldon Square is theirs six weeks later.

The following weekend, it's less foggy and cold. They return to the house and this time go outside the French doors in the only room on the ground floor. Imagine their astonishment when they discover that the house is set cleverly across the front corner of a quarter of an acre – the back garden is huge and totally private for it

FELICITY HERTSLET KAPLAN and her husband bought a house in Reading on impulse 30 years ago, but they did not realise they had also acquired a magical garden. The family has moved on but the memory of the garden remains

is surrounded by a high stone wall. As they are shown round they
see that gates open on to Eldon Terrace. There is a huge plane
tree, an old air raid shelter and masses of trees, shrubs, roses and
other plants, as well as an old greenhouse and a wonderfully large
lawn. They can't all occupy the house till the summer because of
switching schools. But he moves in until the builder's mess becomes
overwhelming and she visits at weekends in an attempt to deal with
the garden. As spring arrives, they realize that they've inherited a
wonderful garden, stocked by experts. But slowly, slowly things
begin to die. She (who knows little about gardening and mostly
does it by instinct) begins to wonder if she's doing something
wrong. After picking and freezing much of a wonderful crop of
Victoria plums they're dismayed to see the tree crumple and die
within days. They ask for advice from a university expert who tells
them that their wonderful secret garden is riddled with *Armillaria
mellea* or the honey fungus.

It strikes at random, attacking anything woody that is in its path.
She tries hard, changing to things like dahlias and vegetables.
Fortunately neither the roses nor a magnolia tree planted in
memory of her mother are attacked.

The family grows up, the garden is used for parties and two
wedding receptions, amazing imaginary games of football are
played on the lawn, wonderful vegetables are produced – the soil is
fabulous since it's on the old town orts. Gardeners come and go,
she gets arthritis, the family disperses and sadly the wonderful space
becomes a burden. After about twenty years we sell and move on.

I long for the courage to go and see what's happened to it.

Romilly Swann

f *for folly court*

The scented memorial garden

Guide dogs are welcome in the scented memorial garden at Folly Court, in Wokingham, and that is as it should be because this garden was designed for them as well as their owners. The ashes of several guide dogs have been scattered within the walled garden and the brass plaques which stud the brickwork tell moving stories of canine fidelity and human devotion.

Here the scent of the flowers is more important than the colours. The garden is in full sunlight for most of the day and with the protection of the surrounding walls the plants have flourished. They bloom earlier than in less sheltered areas and the scents are retained within the garden.

Folly Court, in the aptly named Barkham Road, was bought by the Guide Dogs for the Blind Association in 1975 as the fifth of their seven regional training centres. Before that it had been used as a garden centre and originally was a family home with 95 acres of grounds.

The GDBA demolished some of the derelict buildings on the site and grafted a purpose-built centre to the old house. Only the entrance block and the walled garden are original. Since it was officially opened in May 1977, nearly 2,000 dogs have been trained there as guide dogs. Their importance both as a guide and companion to their owners cannot be overestimated.

An awareness of the close bond between owner and dog and the

There are all kinds of bereavement. When a guide dog dies, its owner loses much more than a pet, it is a life companion, and the period of grieving is often intense. As a lasting memorial to their dogs, a quiet, scented garden at Folly Court, in Wokingham, has been cultivated so that owners can spend a peaceful hour or so smelling the plants and remembering old friends

And because the Breath of Flowers is farre Sweeter in the Aire (where it comes and Goes, like the warbling of Musick) than in the hand, therefore nothing is more fit for that Delight than to know what be the Flowers and plants that doe best perfume the Aire.

**Francis Bacon
Of Gardens**

sense of loss when a guide dog dies were given proper recognition as the result of research carried out by a postgraduate student of the University of Reading for her dissertation. The subject was close to the student's heart because she was one of the GDBA puppywalkers, who care for the young dogs in the early months of their life. She decided to research the effects of bereavement on owners when their guide dogs died and this project revealed the depth of grief many owners had to cope with. The GDBA took action. They now provide counselling for bereaved owners and each centre has a memorial book displayed in which the names and details of guide dogs are permanently recorded.

The idea of a scented memorial garden, as an extension to the memorial books, grew from a chance visit by Ray Smith, public relations manager at Folly Court, to a lecture by Rosemary Campbell-Preston, a gardener from Maidenhead who is a passionate enthusiast of scented plants and aromatic herbs.

The original walled garden at Folly Court was the obvious site but although it had once been used as a rose garden, the area had not been cultivated for several years and was simply a stretch of grass. One quarter of the area was eventually transformed after months of hard work and careful planning.

This was a brickmaking locality and the soil type was marginally acid. Preparatory work was carried out by Peter Harrod, one of the three maintenance staff at Folly Court, and after digging over the new borders, two-and-a-half tons of mushroom compost was added to help water retention and to aerate the soil. This has helped root growth as the plants have become established. Although the compost has helped, the garden still gets very dry so an irrigation system was laid down which operates at night.

Rosemary Campbell-Preston had been invited to view the garden site, became interested in the scheme, and in January 1995 drew up a planting scheme which tried to provide flowers all the year round.

Prospective owners as well as prospective guide dogs are trained at Folly Court which has 104 members of staff. There are some 150 dogs on site at any one time; about 100 dogs are trained a year and, of those, about 65 will be replacements for retired dogs who generally stop working after seven years. GDBA breeds over 1,000 puppies a year to maintain the supply of guide dogs as mobility aids for the visually impaired

In the centre of the garden is an Indian Bean tree underplanted with a succession of bulbs with scented flowers. There are many scented shrubs like viburnum, philadelphus, corylopsis, buddleia, choisya, and rosa, which cut down on maintenance and provide scent at nose level. Even the honeysuckle has been trained up posts so that it blooms at an accessible height. Smaller shrubs and herbaceous plants like lavandula, salvia, dianthus, thymus, convallaria, hosta and viola fill the front of the borders, and, of course, there are many wall-plants, various types of clematis, wisteria, humulus (hops), trachelospermum, jasmine and roses. Rosemary, with the splendid name of Miss Jessop's Upright, surrounds one of the two benches which have been placed there for the use of visitors.

Exotic smells mingle with the sweet fragrance of old-fashioned cottage gardens – chocolate vine and chocolate cosmos, winter sweet, pink lilies-of-the-valley, pineapple broom, bronze fennel, golden hop lemon verbena, french lavender, tobacco plants, old-fashioned roses and the hot smelling curry plant.

The memorial plaques, with messages to 'faithful friends' and 'gentle giants', are displayed all round the walls, and guide dog owners past and present can find comfort in this quiet, sunny and healing place, a walled garden filled with sweet scents and happy memories, where good companions are not forgotten.

Hops by Romilly Swann

f *for fuchsias*

Fascinating fuchsias

More years ago than I care to remember (actually it was in 1964), I chanced upon an advertisement in one of the weekly gardening papers for a collection of a dozen fuchsias. At the time I was looking for plants that would fill a border and, as I was living in Cornwall, I felt that fuchsias might well fit the bill. I remember distinctly that the cost of the collection (including postage) was half a guinea (that is 52p in modern money). In addition I would receive an instructional booklet entitled *Fuchsia Culture*.

Little did I realise then that I would be embarking upon a journey which would give me so much pleasure as well as the opportunity of meeting so many wonderful people.

My fuchsias, being one of the simplest of all plants to grow, flourished. A friend also started to grow fuchsias and as a result we decided to join a newly-formed fuchsia society which met regularly in Plymouth. This proved to be another excellent idea as we were able to listen to experienced growers and pick up ideas for making our plants look even better.

On leaving Cornwall and moving to Reading, I was in limbo for a short while but continued to grow fuchsias and to take an interest in the British Fuchsia Society. In 1974, I decided that a town the size of Reading ought to have its own society. The names of other enthusiasts were obtained through the BFS and Reading and District Fuchsia Society was formed.

For more than 30 years, GEORGE BARTLETT has had a love affair with fuchsias. His fascination with the plant has opened up a new life taking him to the top of the fuchsia world where he was president of the British Fuchsia Society. He still grows fuchsias at his Reading home

My interest in the British Fuchsia Society has prospered and in 1976 I was elected to serve on the committee. A spell as editor of the society publications, a few years in the hot seat as chairman, followed by the privilege of being president of the society for the three years ending 1997, have all helped to strengthen my love of the fuchsia.

But what is it about the fuchsia that is so fascinating? I suppose it is the ease with which it is possible both to grow the plants and to get new plants from older ones, the delightful colouring of the blooms, and the varying ways in which the plants can be displayed (in tubs, in the garden border, in pots, in hanging baskets). All these things make them an enjoyable 'hobby' plant.

No real gardening expertise is necessary to be successful with fuchsias. Any type of multi-purpose compost can be used and success can be assured with a minimum of loving care and attention. Yes, I know that it is possible to grow superb, well-branched, evenly-grown plants suitable for the show bench with a little extra attention, but if you just want a plant that looks nice on the patio then fuchsias are for you.

One word of warning – they can become very addictive and, as there are so many delightful cultivars from which you can choose (more than 8,000 different cultivars), it is sometimes hard to resist the temptation to get just one more.

Let me see if I can whet your appetite just a little. Do you like the feeling of power that emanates from making a new plant from an old plant? If you do, then why not try taking cuttings of fuchsias. It is tempting to say that a hundred-per-cent success can be assured, but there are always those who have a few failures. Fuchsia cuttings will root very easily in a jar of water but unfortunately the root system obtained in water is rather brittle and sometimes losses are experienced when you try to transfer those rooted cuttings into

The Reading and District Fuchsia Society has prospered over the years. An annual show is held and biennially a fuchsia festival. The aim is to encourage as many people as possible to grow fuchsias and to become involved with other like-minded individuals. We are lucky in that there are a number of fuchsia nurseries in the area so it is possible to obtain well-grown and newer varieties.

The society meets on the second and fourth Mondays of each month at 7.30 pm at Reading Girls School, Northumberland Avenue. The fourth Monday in the month is designated as an instructional evening where the basics of growing fuchsias are discussed and demonstrated.

compost. A slight variation though will give you success. A slice from a block of well-soaked Oasis (used by the flower arrangers) is all the equipment you require to root your fuchsias.

Place the Oasis in a saucer and obtain some shoots from fuchsia plants (2 ins to 3 ins long, severed just above the leaf joint). Remove the bottom set of leaves. You will then have a small twig with a couple of pairs of leaves and the growing tip. If the Oasis is very wet, it will probably be possible to push the cuttings into the Oasis but if you prefer, you can make a hole with a piece of flower stick and insert your cutting in that. Insert name labels (if known) alongside the cuttings and then stand the container on a window ledge preferably facing north – we don't really want the hot rays of the sun shining on to the unrooted cuttings. Ensure that the saucer containing the Oasis always has a level of water in it.

After about three weeks you will notice signs of growth in the growing tips. Rooting has started. After another few days it might be possible to see roots coming out of the sides of the Oasis. The time has come to transfer them into a pot containing compost. Separate the cuttings from each other by cutting a core of Oasis around the root system of each young plant. Don't worry about cutting through roots, they will soon grow again. Make sure that when you plant the new plants in their core of Oasis that no part of the Oasis is above the level of the compost. From now onwards these young plants can be treated as you would any other plant, they can be trained and encouraged to branch out by removing the growing tip.

The best time of the year for taking cuttings? Fuchsias will root at any time but perhaps autumn or spring are favourite. Cuttings taken in the autumn from plants growing in the garden can safely be over-wintered on the windowsill. Cuttings taken in the spring will grow away very quickly and will provide good flowering sized plants from July onwards. Have a go. But be warned – Fuchsiamania is a disease which can easily be caught and is hard to cure.

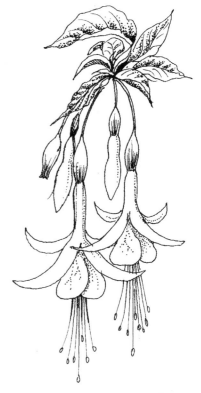

Romilly Swann

g *for garden boy*

The butler brought us fruit cake

In the 1940s most children left school at 14 years of age as I did in 1943. This was still wartime and plenty of jobs were to be had as a large number of grown men were in the forces, so for school-leavers finding work was easy.

My first employment was at Kitford Garden, at East Lockinge near Wantage. My father had worked there for some time and he talked to the head gardener so I was employed as garden boy at £1 per week. This doesn't seem much today – 17 shillings 6d (75p) went for keep to my mother, 6d (2.5p) went towards National Savings Certificates, and the rest, 2 shillings (10p), was for spending on cinema, sweets, and other things.

In those days the staff was a head gardener, three under-gardeners, and two garden boys. The main part of my first job was to bicycle to Lockinge House each morning to take vegetables and fruit and to collect the list of vegetables wanted by the cook the next day. This bicycle had a small wheel at the front with a basket in a frame on top.

One job I hated was picking up apple prunings which after night frost or light snow were very cold to your hands, also to your feet. Another job was washing flower pots (not the plastic ones of today). Once Leslie, the other garden boy, loaded them up in a wheelbarrow and managed to tip the lot over, so we spent quite a bit of time clearing up broken pieces.

REG RHODES

REG RHODES, who now lives in Thatcham, started work when he was only 14 and apart from one short spell spent the rest of his working life as a gardener. He reminisces about life as garden boy in Berkshire half a century ago

Another time I remember going to pick a nice juicy pear that had fallen from a tree against a wall. My father saw me eating it and asked where I got it from. I told him and he said all those pears had been counted, so he went to the orchard to get a similar one and placed it by the tree. As far as I know no one was any the wiser.

Remembering those days brings back happy memories – wheel hoes, painting the cuts on the grape vines after pruning to stop bleeding, disbudding the carnations in the carnation houses, spraying the peach trees with water to avoid red spider. There was not much in the way of insecticide in those days. Pesticides were mainly soft soap and nicotine.

We carried barrows of straw and if you dropped any you had to pick up every tiny bit. I remember the huge chrysanthemums, about 6ft high with huge blooms each like a ball. The young garden boys had to carry them and it would be more than your life's worth if you dropped one.

There were no electric hedge-trimmers or machines for cutting long grass. All this was done by hand. I still believe that hedges can be cut better by hand shears. I never use anything else. My father told me never to learn to use a scythe. I have tried but each scythe has to be set to the individual.

Alas, Kitford Garden is no longer gardens and Lockinge House was pulled down years ago although Lockinge is still the sleepy village it was then. My parents moved from Lockinge to East Woodhay, near Newbury, towards the end of the war. My father worked at Stargroves, later Mick Jagger's home, and I got a job at Malverlys, East Woodhay, cycling to work and back home at lunch time. It was still wartime and again labour was in short supply.

The head gardener, and his brother, two others and myself were the staff at Malverlys. This garden, despite the shortages, was kept to a high standard. We spent hours digging daisies from the lawns, and days weeding the terraces between the paving stones. On nice sunny afternoons the butler used to come from the house with large cups of tea and lumps of fruit cake sent out by the owners. In later years people who I've worked for didn't bother about things like that. You would be wasting time.

Petrol was short in those days so cutting lawns was difficult. We got over this by getting a pony to pull the machine, the chauffeur steering and myself leading the pony.

When the war came to an end, the people in the forces came home and went back to gardening. We had National Service then and I had to go and do my 18-month stint. One job I did annually before I went in the Army was to go in the meadows with a hessian sack to collect dried cow pats. These were mixed with soot and placed in a barrel, sack and all, and filled with water to make a liquid manure diluted with water to feed the arum lilies and other plants.

I remember being given a weeding job by the head gardener which I had finished quite quickly. More weeds were close nearby which I started pulling up. The head gardener asked what I was doing as he had not told me to pull them up. I said I thought they needed doing and I was told I was not paid to think. Could one get away with that Victorian attitude today?

Anyhow, I finished my National Service and went to another job at Ball Hill, Newbury. Two elderly gentlemen were employed there and we were growing vegetables to be taken to hotels. I was 22 then and I left there as I wanted a rise. I was offered 2 shillings 6d (12.5p) so I found a job working on my own for an elderly couple. I stayed for some time until the gentleman died and the house was sold. I stayed on with the new owner and was there for some while.

I took a few years out from gardening to sell insurance but finished that after six years to go back to working as a self-employed gardener. I enjoyed being independent but winter times were hard and people were not keen on paying if you could not work. I returned to full-time gardening and worked for a man whose son had

If your peas are getting eaten by mice, plant with holly or gorse on top of them. Mice will not touch them when they prick their noses.

Reg Rhodes

died tragically. I worked with him for some years. He was a very good gentleman and I learned a lot from him. His lawn had no moss or weeds because each year he sprinkled neat soot on the lawn and always timed it when it was going to rain and it was washed in. I tried this once and it didn't rain so I finished up with bare patches where it had burnt. The trouble with this method was when the owners got a dog, it picked up soot on its feet and took it indoors, so this practice stopped.

I eventually got married and wanted a house to live in so I found work at Compton Newbury which had a house with the job. So for 27 years, until I retired at 65, I stayed at that job. Perhaps, on reflection, if it was not for the house, I might have left earlier as more and more pressure was being put on and the standard getting harder to maintain (and the standard was very high). But when you have nowhere else to live you have to put up with it.

I still enjoy gardening today and like to take an overgrown garden to clear. It's a challenge and fun and that's what it should be.

When it's not, give up.

THE GLORY OF THE GARDEN

Our England is a garden that is full of stately views,
Of borders, beds and shrubberies and lawns and avenues,
With statues on the terraces and peacocks strutting by;
But the Glory of the Garden lies in more than meets the eye.

For where the old thick laurels grow, along the thin red wall,
You find the tool- and potting-sheds which are the heart of all;
The cold-frames and the hot-houses, the dungpits and the tanks,
The rollers, carts and drain-pipes. with the barrows and the planks.

And there you'll see the gardeners, the men and 'prentice boys
Told off to do as they are bid and do it without noise;
For, except when seeds are planted and we shout to scare the birds,
The Glory of the Garden it abideth not in words.

And some can pot begonias and some can bud a rose,
And some are hardly fit to trust with anything that grows;
But they can roll and trim the lawns and sift the sand and loam,
For the Glory of the Garden occupieth all who come.

Our England is a garden, and such gardens are not made
By singing: "Oh, how beautiful!" and sitting in the shade,
While better men than we go out and start their working lives
At grubbing weeds from gravel-paths with broken dinner-knives.

From The Glory of the Garden
Rudyard Kipling

Gone with the wind

I was born and bred in the country and that was my life. I didn't have a very good education – I used to have to walk two miles to elementary school when I was five and I left at 14. I went to work for a vicar, the Revd Fosbroke Hobbes, at Ashbury, as a sort of jack-of-all-trades. Eventually I took over the garden. I was self-taught but nobody could be keener on gardening than I am. I don't like to brag but people would come to the garden and say, 'How many gardeners do they employ here?' and when I said, 'Oh, I do it all,' they wouldn't believe me. It came naturally to me, but it's been my great regret in life that I didn't have a basic training in gardening. I learned to garden chiefly by doing it, though I've always bought gardening books. I think you can learn from books if you are really keen.

The Revd Fosbroke Hobbes, a descendant of the philosopher Thomas Hobbes, was originally in the army, but later became a clergyman. When he moved to South Ascot to take over the living of the parish, I went with him. It was here that I met my future wife.

I was a very eligible man of 27 and any amount of girls set their sights on me but they didn't appeal to me. Then I saw this girl, Olive, in church and I was attracted to her, I can't explain it. I had been a little bit friendly with her sister and she invited me home for Christmas. When I turned up who should I meet but the girl I had seen in church. She told me her sister had decided she wouldn't come down. She'd gone off me because I wore boots! Olive didn't mind the boots and we married 18 months afterwards.

The vicar wasn't in a position to pay me enough money to keep a wife, so I moved to Whitchurch, Pangbourne, and was there for about three years, when the family came along.

After the war, in 1947 I went to work for Page's, a big nursery specialising in growing carnations, in Winkfield Row. They had four or five acres of glass in Winkfield Row and another eight acres of

There can be few gardeners as keen as 87-year-old JOE SIMPSON, of South Ascot, who has spent a lifetime working in gardens, visiting gardens, and enjoying gardens

Drawing by Olive Simpson

69

glass near Hampton Court. Now it's all gone with the wind. The Suez crisis put paid to that. The price of oil went up and up and the glasshouses in this country couldn't compete.

During the war, Page's were only allowed to keep a certain amount of carnations to keep the stocks going and they went into growing tomatoes. As the war finished they reverted to what they specialised in – growing perpetual flowering carnations. During the main season in July, they were sending up 1,000 boxes of carnations a day to Covent Garden – and you could get three dozen in each box – and at night they would send hundreds more.

They employed a lot of people: four regularly in the packing shed, four women in each glasshouse, which were one acre in extent, and a man in charge of each glasshouse. During the summer they employed part-timers to help with the disbudding and the packing.

I started on the boilers and eventually I became a chargehand in one of the blocks which grew carnations. I enjoyed that, it was in my blood. I was at Page's for 25 years and then the carnations came to an end. After a short spell with a mushroom grower, I retired at 65

What do I think is the secret of gardening? It's all in the soil. A garden is like a bank balance – it's what you put into it. If you don't put anything into it, you won't get anything out of it.

Our soil here in Ascot is very light and sandy but not far away, the soil is heavy clay. The reason you have this variation is that the Bagshot sands meet the London clays , so you have to think what will grow best. It's an acid soil so it's ideal for rhododendrons, azaleas, and camellias. Look at the Valley Gardens and Savill Garden, in Windsor Great Park. Personally I've found shrubs seem to do very well indeed, they like the drainage. You have got to start from basics and grow the things according to the soil you have got.

by Olive Simpson

'My wife was one of a family of 12, eight girls and four boys. She used to cycle from Sunninghill to Staines where she worked and she was paid £1 a week. In the winter she was permitted to travel on the train. She was an extraordinary person, very keen on writing and painting. I think she deserved more recognition. We had over 50 happy years together, and travelled miles to see gardens and garden shows, first on bicycles, later by car.'
Joe Simpson

g for grazeley school

Our Victorian garden

Our school is hoping to make a Victorian garden. We will use Victorian plants and trees because we have studied the Victorians and our school is Victorian.

The Victorians had some very lovely flowers, which we will use. Our front garden is going to be transformed with a passage through the middle and vines hanging down from the walls. There are plans to make seed beds, circular and straight.

We do not, however, have the huge amount and variety of Victorian plants, as the Victorians went to far-away countries to collect their specimens. As many people went abroad for education, plants were brought back from the continent, especially Italy. Between 1840 and 1860 thousands of new plants took root in Britain. Gardening had never been so exciting! The Victorians loved colourful flower beds. We would like to plant our own beds here at Grazeley. The colourful plants would brighten the school and be enjoyed by everyone.

How plants got here

The Victorians did not have many plants in their gardens. They decided to grow more flowers in their gardens but where would they get them from? They could not bring seeds because they did not have the right conditions to grow them. They could bring plants in pots, but they would die from the salt water. A person called Mr

History came alive for the children of GRAZELEY PAROCHIAL PRIMARY SCHOOL, in Grazeley, Reading, when the whole school – staff, pupils and parents – became involved in a project to recreate a Victorian garden there in 1996. The school itself is Victorian and was founded in 1861, which gave the project a special relevance. Tom Brigden, Henry Cockburn, Victoria Taylor, Susie Gillis and the children of Class Two tell the story

Ward invented some miniature greenhouses for each plant. It had wood at the bottom of it where the soil was and glass round the plant. It was called a Wardian.

The people of the town had to build a big greenhouse because some of the plants came from very hot countries so some needed warmth more than others. It was called a conservatory. It would be the gardeners' job to look after the plants.

Our main feature is the garden outside the library. We plan to construct a pergola across the library wall. This would be draped with vines and creepers. This would create shade for the pupils in the hot sun. From here we would have a path to the centre of the garden. Here we have planted a crab-apple tree which, when fully grown, will also give gentle shade across the grass. Going from here two paths would cut across the grass to either side of the lavender hedge, which we have already planted.

Across one edge of the garden would be a semi-circular bed, where there will be a variety of herbs: borage, chives, lemon balm, creeping thyme, sage and parsley. Across the front wall of the library we have a cherry tree. We will trim the bed with bergenia. In this bed will be many flowers such as bluebells. We will be planting other beds around the school as well. We have to remember positions of plants: some plants may like to face north and some south, some may like shade and some may not.

So we must plan everything thoroughly before the planting stage.

Victorian plants and flowers

The well-known bluebell is Victorian but it was around before Victorian times. The bluebell grows under trees because of the shade. The Victorians used bluebells in their gardens because they liked pretty things and bluebells were pretty. The Victorians had the rose, for the rose was the queen of the garden and Victorian gardeners liked roses because they smelled wonderful and they

'I like an Alexander Rose because it is red and a rose is my best flower and I like the name Alexander because it sounds kind. I would like to be in the back garden with all the roses everywhere but different names and colours that I like.'

THE FLOWERS OF THE YEAR

Spring flower,
Spring flower,
Round the bend,
When will your glory end?

Summer flower,
Summer flower,
Happy,
Full of life!

Autumn flower,
Autumn flower,
Leaves falling down,
Twirling, twirling to the ground.

Winter flower,
Winter flower,
You are bare
But here comes the sun!

Victoria Taylor

looked nice in the garden. They can be seen in flower beds or climbing up walls and trellises.

Herbs

Lavender, sage, thyme, mint and parsley were some very lovely herbs. The Victorians were very keen on them. They used the herbs for cooking, making the place smell nice and for things like that. Camomile was a very popular herb and they would make camomile tea and even biscuits! Catmint has grey leaves and misty-blue flowers in the summer.

I think this plant is very pretty because it is purple and tall and purple will look pretty in the sun.

Bees will be very attracted to the plant so I think it will be good to put in the garden.

Delphinium by Class Two

GARDEN WISDOM

The most useful piece of gardening advice given to me as a novice was probably this: if you're really busy, behind and not sure what to do first, get your seeds grown. Other jobs can be tackled later, but sowing-dates are often crucial and it's easy to miss the boat. This was given to me by a very experienced foreman propagator when I was an assistant gardener in the nurseries at Hall Place, London Borough of Bexley. The most useful tip I would give to a beginner now is: many projects begin with plot clearance. The only trouble is, cleared ground often grows over again while your back is turned. When an area is completed, cover with black polythene or even plant potatoes in it to keep the ground clean while moving on to the next. Most plants take best when planted during autumn.
Anne Swithinbank

h *for hamstead marshall*

A garden fit for a Queen

One of the great gardens of Berkshire was created in the Stuart period for the Earl of Craven at Hamstead Marshall. For several centuries the Cravens were one of Berkshire's most powerful families. William, first Earl of Craven, did not marry although he is remembered for his romantic attachment to King James I's daughter, the ex-Queen of Bohemia. Over ninety at the time of his death, he had an eventful life and was in command of English forces involved in the Thirty Years War in Central Europe. This brought him into close contact with European Royalty and raised the status of the Craven family. During the Civil War in this country, he gave financial help to the King.

To reflect the increased prestige and connections of the family, the building at Hamstead Marshall of a vast mansion house, with large formal gardens and long avenues, was put in hand.

Planned by Balthazar Gerbier (who is buried in the church) on the scale of a royal palace, it was built between 1662 and 1686. The features of this great domain included alleys of ornamental trees and a number of small lakes and artificial brooks, all on flat land to the south of the Kennet

The pleasure garden, recorded in the engravings of the 18th century artist Kip, had hedged plots, each with its clipped corner tree, intersected by broad paths. In front of the house was a huge circular bed, divided up like the points of a compass. At the west end

The spectacular garden and mansion of Hamstead Marshall, created for an exiled Queen by the man who loved her all his life, no longer exist but there still remains an intriguing story of a mysterious marble statue which has disappeared and reappeared over the centuries. TONY BARHAM traces its story

of the church, which still exists, was a double row of square vegetable plots separated by paths.

The first Earl devoted years of his life to the service of Elizabeth Stuart, the ex-Queen of Bohemia, and an explanation of the great expense lavished on the estate may be that he intended it to become the home of the exiled Queen.

The splendid mansion had a short life, though it attracted many visitors in the years of its existence. It was destroyed by fire in 1718. No attempt was made to rebuild but a smaller house (surviving as Hamstead Lodge) was erected nearby in 1720.

Eight pairs of entrance piers remain from the old mansion and these help to give the gardens some feeling of the former grandeur.

Another intriguing feature of the garden also appeared to escape the fire. About the year 1885, a dealer in antiques, who claimed to be acting for a Mr Dalrymple, asked a reputable London auction house to dispose of a marble statue. It depicted a girl of about ten or eleven years of age and, according to the dealer, "… stood for many years at the far end of an alley of exotic trees at Hamstead Marshall, an old seat of the Earls of Craven in Berkshire."

The statue had, it seems, once been thought to portray Ruperta, the illegitimate daughter of Prince Rupert of the Rhine (of Civil War fame) but evidence had come to light that it had been acquired at Naples during the 18th century. Expert opinion was that the girl was not Ruperta but a German princess who went on to have a private life which was lurid and sensational. It was supposed to have been brought to Hamstead Marshall from Combe Abbey, a former Craven estate near Coventry (and, as it happens, the place where Elizabeth Stuart spent most of her childhood.)

As the dealer was not of the highest repute, the auctioneers made further inquiries and learned that the statue had come into the

THE VEILED LADY

There is a legend that a heavily veiled, unnamed lady gave birth to a healthy daughter at Hamstead Marshall in 1575. The midwife who had been procured In London watched in horror as the child was thrown on the fire by its putative father, one Wild William Dayrell. The midwife died of poison a few days later but not before naming the mother as Queen Elizabeth I. The story is told in *Kennet Country* by Fred S Thacker, who moved the location from Littlecote to Hamstead Marshall. The supposed source is a letter of 1601 from William Knyght, in Hanover, reporting rumours put about by Hugh Broughton, who had a grudge against the queen.

hands of Mr Dalrymple in rather odd, and even suspicious, circumstances. A document of sale was produced which purported to have been signed, as agent, by a steward who had formerly been employed by a Dowager Countess of Craven but had left her service at the time the document was dated. Because of this, the auction house refused to handle the statue and it was later sold privately.

In 1906 it came to light in the yard of a Fulham dealer who, it is said, offered to sell it back to the Craven family for £60.

Although the value of the statue was probably much greater than this amount, the then Earl, not unreasonably, objected to paying £60 for what was, in all probability, his own property. Legal steps were then taken to recover the old statue but action was delayed for several months and the statue vanished once again, and this time it seems to have gone for good.

Hamstead Marshall from the engraving by Kip

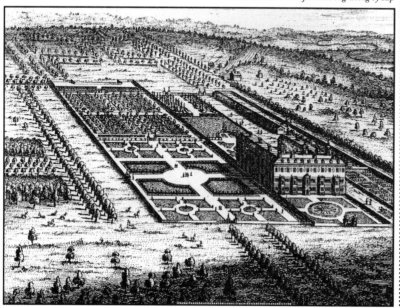

HAIKU AND SENRYU

sickly yellow grass
where the planks lay all winter
an image persists

in the sun's last rays
suddenly shivering –
from the North cold air

white cherry blossom
turns out to be apple –
an easy mistake

almost forgotten
in the longer grass
tiny blue flowers

still without leaves
the tree in the garden

a heron flies over
a few branches of blossom
seen between pines

yellow-black pansies
flower between rhubarb leaves

among the forget-me-nots –
goose droppings

carrying his shoes
an old man walks on the grass –
a Buddha at heart

Mike Facherty

h *for harris garden*

Seeds of learning

The history of university botanic gardens goes back to Luca Ghini's garden in Pisa, established in 1543. The first in England was founded at Oxford in 1621 and the second (just after Edinburgh's) was in 1673: the Chelsea Physic Garden. Both still occupy their original sites and were 'physic gardens', established as an adjunct to medical studies, as were most of the early examples.

The pattern of the physic garden is based on the monastic garden, so the first example in Reading was undoubtedly at the Abbey. When Ellis Peters wished Brother Cadfael to entertain a fellow-herbalist (in *The Pilgrim of Hate*), it seems entirely appropriate that Brother Adam should be from Reading Abbey. Note also that he returned home with seeds of species his garden did not yet possess, for seed exchange has long been a function of gardens established for scholarly purposes. The transmission of learning and the means of learning, both down the generations and from place to place, is a function common to monasteries and universities. Even the modern science of genetics was conceived in Mendel's monastery garden.

However the University Extension College, Reading, was in 1892 on a town centre site with no garden. They soon made an arrangement with Sutton and Sons for the use of their trial grounds, containing 'plots of all the grasses and forage plants and trial plots of different grass seed mixtures'. By the turn of the century classes in horticulture, leading to a joint Oxford and Reading Certificate, then

The Harris Garden, at the University of Reading, named after a former Professor of Botany, follows in a long and honoured tradition of university botanic gardens as DERMOT O'ROURKE explains

a Diploma, were well established.

Alfred Palmer had provided the college with a site in London Road which included a four-acre garden, soon to be supplied with potting and packing sheds, office and laboratory, greenhouses and a peach house, vineries (early and late), together with vegetable, fruit and flower gardens and bee-hives. Contemporary photographs show all this with the familiar Great Hall in the background, and another aspect of it occurs with a rose garden in the foreground observed from near the spot where Gyosei College's Friendship Gate now stands. In addition the two-acre garden of nearby Saint Andrew's Hall was 'available for practical work by women students', presumably in addition to access to the main gardens since women may well have been in the majority. Early in the century horticulture was seen as a suitable occupation for young ladies.

In 1903 the college had acquired Lane End Farm in Shinfield for agricultural teaching. By 1917 pressure on space at London Road caused the horticultural garden to be re-established at Shinfield and later this became the garden for the Agricultural Botany Department when Shinfield Grange, the other side of Cutbush Lane from the Farm, was acquired for the Horticulture Department. The existence of these two departments reflects the university's long-standing leaning towards the applied biological sciences. The pure science of botany was of course taught but practical work rarely needed a garden.

By 1972 the Departments of Botany and of Agricultural Botany moved to a new building in Whiteknights and established a botanic garden nearby, with adjacent experimental grounds. When in 1987 the Department of Horticulture joined them to form the School of Plant Sciences, the garden was expanded. Appropriately it now included a site marked in an 1840s plan as Chantilly Garden, modelled on Le Nôtre's garden at the château there.

The garden has been named after Tom Harris, FRS, Professor of

The plant sciences building

Botany from 1934 to 1968, an authority on fossil plants and a keen gardener, who died in 1983. It has public open days, and members of the public are encouraged to join the Friends of the Harris Garden which allows them free access at other times as well as other benefits.

The garden occupies about 12 acres with some fifteen distinct areas to provide interest throughout the year. A Winter Garden and the borders near the entrance display winter-flowering shrubs and plants with attractive foliage, bark or berries. In the Spring one might visit the orchard for the bulbs and wild flowers beneath ornamental crab-apples, the Cherry Bowl for its Japanese flowering cherries, the Woodland Garden (site of the 1970s botanic garden) with bluebells, wood anemones and celandines, and the Primula Dell.

The Great Hall viewed from the horticultural garden which was soon to be built upon

The foliage border and annual borders are planted out in May/June; there is a rose garden and formal gardens with a re-creation of Gertrude Jekyll's famous flower border at Munstead Wood, illustrating her ideas on colour planning. The scale of the garden does mean that there is nothing, alas, to match the 300-ft laburnum tunnel that existed here in the early 19th century! However, the foliage border is planted each June with a range of annual and tender plants popular in Victorian times for their 'sub-tropical' effect, with some of them growing to spectacular heights considering that they were raised from seed the same year.

The orchard is again colourful with foliage and fruit, and there is an autumn bank beyond the pond. Fruit and vegetables are grown in the traditional walled garden, where there is also a herb garden bringing us full circle to the medicinal and culinary origins of the botanic garden. The herbarium in the Botany Department still circulates lists of seeds for exchange with other botanic gardens.

Bunty Nash, a student at the University of Reading during the Second World War, recalls Professor Harris popping out to the ornamental garden alongside the Great Hall to pick plants for identification and description in a practical examination. She remembers a cycle ride to Burghfield as an example of the forays on which the students learned about wild flowers, and also recalls with enduring enthusiasm one field trip to Westmorland with the Botanical Society on which they learned as much about the geology of the landscape as of the flora.

h for hedges

Hedging tips

Privet hedge – *Ligustrum ovalifolium.* Evergreen. Grows fast to any height. Makes a good screen. Planting Oct.–April. Propagated by cuttings. Cut hard May –August. Golden privet is more attractive.

Beech hedge – *Fagus sylvatica.* Semi deciduous. Slow growing for two years then medium growth. Lime green leaves in spring and hangs on to copper-coloured leaves in winter. Planting Oct.–March. Propagated from seedlings. Trim July–August.

Yew hedge – *Taxus baccata.* Evergreen. Excellent, slow-growing hedge used in topiary. Gold tipped species very attractive. Plant March–May or Sept.–Oct. Trim June–July. Clippings used for cancer research.

Box hedge – *Buxus sempervirens.* Evergreen. Attractive small hedge for edging garden beds. No more than 1ft high. Slow growing. Can be used in topiary. Plant Oct.–Nov. or April–May. If trimmed too late will not survive winter frosts, so trim June (preferably Derby week!)

Conifer hedge – x *Cupressocyparis leylandii.* Evergreen. Modern-day hedge. Fast growing. Plant Oct.–Nov. or April–May. Trim May–June.

Rosemary – *Rosmarinus officinalis.* Evergreen. Medium growth. Attractive scented hedge. Plant Sept.–Oct. or March–April. Trim lightly July–August.

Holly – *Ilex aquifolium.* Evergreen. Attractive hedge with berries, ideal for deterring would-be trespassers! Slow growing. Plant April–May or Sept.—Oct. Trim in July.

TED KELLY started as a gardener and worked at the Royal Botanic Gardens at Kew. He now engraves plant labels for Savill Garden in Windsor Great Park

Some other species for hedging are:
Berberis darwinii – attractive foliage, evergreen.
Chamaecyparis lawsoniana – evergreen.
Queen Elizabeth rose – pink roses, heavily scented.
Lavender (*Lavandula*) – attractive, heavily scented.

h *for herbalist*

Magic in the garden

Sage is for wisdom! I have it on good authority. Lilian Skeels, a psychic mediator, healer, tarot card reader, creator of gardens, and definitely a wise woman, recommends breathing in the aroma of sage or gently brushing your arms and legs with sprigs of the herb as a way of keeping the brain healthy and the imagination creative.

Lilian is an expert in myth and legend, and familiar with the language of flowers – bleeding heart for sympathy, one red rose for love, three for 'I Love You', white lilac for misfortune and so on. But she points out that many old wives' tales and much plant lore is based on good sense.

Cow parsley for example is said to be unlucky. It also looks very similar to the deadly poisonous hemlock, so is best not picked, just in case. And while picking dandelions may not actually make you wet the bed, dandelion tea is in fact a strong diuretic. Lilian also suggests eating honeysuckle flowers to cure, and then prevent, hayfever.

She says many such 'magic' properties of plants are suggested by the plants themselves and it was when she was discussing a friend's hayfever with him that she caught sight of the honeysuckle through the window and it said, "Here I am!" And the idea that they should each eat two bunches of the flowers to keep them immune for two years was suggested to her. They did – and it worked. She has since recommended this to many friends, with a 98 per cent success rate, and she herself takes a regular nibble of the petals to keep the allergy

SUSAN UTTING meets an extraordinary woman living in a Bracknell housing estate who not only talks to the flowers, but listens to what they say to her. This wise woman believes in the magic properties of all growing things and is sure that there are spiritual links between people and plants

Sage

at bay. Asked if it tastes nice, she replied, "Not brilliant!"

It is commonly accepted that plants benefit from being talked to, but Lilian also firmly believes that flowers and plants talk to us as they grow – and we can learn and benefit from them. She says that gardens must be full of magic – and useful knowledge – because plants and all growing things are rich with nature's life force at its strongest and most innocent.

Lilian moved from a mobile home in an ancient woodland setting, dense with wild plants and wildlife, to a terrace on a Bracknell housing estate, where I met her. From the front the contrast is sharp – here there's hardly a bit of green to relieve the brick-built row; but through the house and out of the french windows at the back there's a tiny patch of magic. What Lilian describes as 'like a bomb site' when she arrived, has been transformed into a lush and richly growing garden full of climbing plants, (yes – honeysuckle), herbs, shrubs and flowers that look as if they've been there for generations. They have responded to her and flourish here.

For Lilian believes plants listen and understand, and know our intentions. Before we pick flowers, or start weeding or bruising, pruning or mowing – or uprooting – she recommends we simply stand and look for a moment. The growing things will know our good intentions, prepare themselves, and respond to treatment. Charge in like a bull at a garden gate and they scream with fear and wither. This empathy between plants and those who tend them works both ways. One tiny plant with heart-shaped flowers actually died at the time that Lilian split up with her partner. But as she recovered from the pain of this and started to gather strength and grow from the experience, the plant, too,

OLD WIVES' TALE

And the wise old woman said:
"Sage is for wisdom
beat your limbs with it, gently
till the smell of it rises
and your skin is dusty
as a dusk moth's wing.

Honeysuckle's for a long life
steep its dawn picked petals to a tea
sip it slow, one thoughtful throatful
at a time till its flavours, all petal-sweet
and scented have sugared your tongue.

For fecundity there's crabapples
and cider apple vinegar, the sourest
juices from a quince and the mouth-cruel
rinds of an orange, or the bitter thick
skin of a cucumber stub."

And her children came,
and her children's children,
and her children's children's children,
and theirs, all came together and laughed
and danced and laughed and knew and lived.

Susan Utting

started to revive and put out new shoots.

This idea of the spiritual connections between plants and people, and in particular the transference of life force from plants to people and vice versa, is again demonstrated in one corner of Lilian's garden that does seem to be more rich with colour, more dense with shades of green, more lush and vibrant than the rest. In amongst this specially fast-growing patch is a strange assortment of clay pots – push aside a clump of Michaelmas daisies and there's a fairy tale castle, over there between the golden rod and the marguerites there's a strange figure – an old man's face, a frog?

These pots are the magic ingredients, a legacy bequeathed to Lilian by a friend who was a potter, a poet – and a skilful gardener – whose illness had been put into remission by Lilian's healing. She believes it is his spirit, his influence through the gift of these artefacts he created, that lives on in her garden and encourages it to thrive.

One of Lilian's 'magic' clay pots

In amongst these magical ornaments, sometimes lit by nightlights, one could almost imagine seeing small people, and Lilian is a firm believer in fairies. She says that every plant and flower has its own spiritual companion, and this is the origin of the little people. Fairy legends exist in many cultures, and fairies are most commonly seen in garden and woodland settings. And while Lilian admits that there have been many hoaxes, she claims that just as many true sightings of fairies are not spoken about for fear of sounding foolish.

Though she herself has never seen one except in a dream state, her mother, whom she describes as a very down-to- earth and ordinary woman, and therefore to be believed, once did. She, together with a friend, saw two fairies mending the broken stem of a daffodil with twine. And while I didn't actually come across any of the little people in Lilian's garden, there definitely does seem to be a lot of natural magic at work there.

Pining to be among the trees again, Lilian has since moved back to her mobile home. I suspect she has taken her magic with her.

h *for hurst bowling green*

'A large and handsome bowling green'

Greenkeeping is an art and it can also be a religion as the 'three wise men' of Hurst Bowling Club – its unpaid but devoted greenkeepers – can testify. As the club celebrates its 250th anniversary this year (1997), despite drought, anno domini and the lurking dangers of disease, the green is still a picture. It has needed to stand up to much wear and tear in its anniversary year because there have been 84 matches, more than ever before, but when the county inspectors came to ensure it met county competition standards, it passed with flying colours.

Tradition says that the bowling green at Hurst is the second oldest in the south of England but much of its history is conjecture since an unhelpful person consigned the club's records to the bonfire. It is believed the green was first laid in the 17th century, about 1628, when Hurst was part of Windsor Great Park. It is quite feasible it could have been laid either for Charles I, a keen bowls player, or possibly his son Charles II. What is certain is that the club was founded in 1747 and took its emblem, a bunch of grapes, from the name of the adjacent pub (now called The Castle).

Its most distinguished visiting player was Dr W G Grace, the famous cricketer, who brought a team to Hurst in May 1905, and was beaten 77 to 46. In August, he returned for revenge with a team stuffed with internationals but the game ended in a tie, 56 shots each. Two copies of hand-written letters about the event from the

Bowling is, next to archery, the oldest British outdoor pastime still played and has been traced back to the 13th century. There are 52 affiliated clubs in Berkshire and one of them, HURST BOWLING CLUB, is celebrating its 250th anniversary. However its bowling green goes back even further and the care and condition of this historic green rests with three devoted club members

good doctor hang in the clubhouse.

Three years after this, in 1908, the green was relaid and nearly 90 years later is still 'running' well. Since Sydney Clarke, who is 80, Reg Prickett, 76, and Harold Poole, 66, took over the care of the green it has flourished. The secret, they say, is "love, care and attention". This attention is needed round the year and can take about 20 hours a week. They have been known to go to the green at 4.30 in the morning to check the water sprinklers.

It's a beautiful green and although not quite square, and not quite full size (about 39 yards rather than 42 yards) it is still well within the regulations. When Sydney became unpaid greenkeeper in 1988, joined a couple of years later by Reg and then Harold, the green was weedy and seriously worn. Rinks should be moved about twice a week so the green gets worn evenly but this had not been done for years and their first job was to level out the undulation in the surface by injecting the hollows with sand. (The six rinks are now moved regularly.) Another major task was lifting the edges which had spread with wear and run right off the green. This also entailed rebuilding the banks and finishing off with 40 tons of topsoil (about 500 separate loads) which had to be levelled.

To ensure players have a good, running green there must be a constant programme of weed and disease control, scarification, aeration, feeding, mowing, rolling and watering. The greenkeepers' year starts in September when the playing season ends.

"First we thoroughly

In 1747 a Mr Belchin described in his diary how, after morning service at the parish church opposite, he had visited Church House (the church-owned licensed property). "This house is very pleasantly situated and has belonging to it a very large and handsome bowling green for the diversion of those gentlemen who are pleased to play."

The doctor takes charge. Dr W G Grace (the tall bearded figure) with his team at Hurst

scarify the grass, removing about 20 barrow loads of rubbish," said Reg, "then we spike it, using solid and hollow tines to aerate the surface. We sow about half a hundredweight of special grass seed, followed by four tons of top dressing, seven parts Leighton Buzzard sand to three parts sterilised loam. This is spread evenly, using a 9ft long frame which is pulled across the green at an angle of 30 degrees. Fertiliser is applied – then we pray for rain!"

The grass is mown during this period with a cut raised to five-eights. (Very different from the days when the green was cut by a horse-drawn mower with the horse wearing straw-stuffed bootees so as not to mark the surface.)

A constant lookout is kept for some of the unpleasant fungal diseases (with names like pink snow patch, brown patch, and golden spot) which can play havoc with the greens. They are contagious and can be carried from green to green but fortunately Hurst has escaped. However they have had problems keeping the greens watered during the recent dry summers because their water system is antiquated and is not helped by the variable water pressure.

In the spring, work continues with light scarifying and rolling, and spiking and the cut on the mower is gradually lowered from half an inch to three-sixteenths of an inch. When the dew is on the grass in the morning, a big brush is dragged across against the cut, to knock off the dew. Nothing is left to chance. The three men keep checking the green day by day. It becomes obsessive, they admit, and Harold says comments are passed at home about the state of his own garden.

During the whole of the playing season, there is a programme of regular spiking, scarifying and fertilizing, with watering as required, mowing at least three times a week, and selective weed killing when needed. The bowling must come as light relief!

Hurst is a small private club with no extra funding so the money it costs for the upkeep of the green – nearly £2,000 a year – comes from the fees of the 60 members. There is little left for anything else and the 100-year-old clubhouse is modest in the extreme. A long-running battle with the local church over ownership of the land means the club cannot press ahead with building plans.

The three wise men of Hurst Bowling Club (left to right) Harold Poole, Reg Prickett and Sydney Clarke

i for informal gardens

No such things as weeds

I think the important thing for me is that when people talk about gardening – what is a garden and what isn't a garden – one person's idea of attractiveness is often completely at odds with someone else's. If you look at what people did 20 years ago, the general idea was formal borders with plants planted out evenly with a ruler to make them exactly six inches apart; there'd be straight edges down the sides of the lawn edged with a special edging tool. The grass would be cut, and so-called weeds would be killed. Loads of water would be used to keep it an artificial green colour. Now we have moved quite a long way from that, and there are very few people who actually keep formal gardens.

There are probably lots of reasons for that – one is that we don't have the time any more, and also it makes it so formal that people feel they can't even walk in the garden for fear of upsetting something. We've moved away from the straight edges and the symmetrical garden and now people have got wavy meandering edges and they have shrubberies which are low-management. They don't have to go out every weekend and trim and weed. They put down mulches like woodchips between the plants.

When I took over my garden the grass was regularly cut all over, and the bushes were kept cut back but it was basically a lawn with a little strip of soil where nothing much happened. What I've done on part of the lawn is to plant herbs in a sunny position, and I've planted

RAY HARRINGTON-VAIL

RAY HARRINGTON-VAIL is a park ranger with Earley Town Council, who believes strongly in low-management, informal gardens. He talks about his own ideas on gardening and his plans to create a small 'tribute garden' to the memory of Geoff Hamilton, the BBC gardening expert

a buddleia so that it also attracts butterflies. Cutting herbs encourages them to grow and keeps them healthy – it's desirable, functional and a self-perpetuating use of land. You can harvest without harming things, and herbs are a prime example. If you don't cut sage down every so many years it goes woody and dies, a bit like a willow tree. It actually benefits a willow tree to be cut back, it stops it getting top heavy and falling over.

Most herbs are pretty easy to grow, and are Mediterranean in origin and therefore they like sunlight, and don't like much water. So you haven't to worry, 'Oh well, I'm going on holiday for a week, all my herbs are going to die'. Most herbs – thyme, sage, rosemary – are not going to die from lack of watering.

I deliberately leave a little bit of grass to grow long and put in a wild flower mix. This piece of land is only 3 ft by 3ft in size, but it's a mini meadow with a buddleia behind it, so you've got a mixture there of native wild flowers and buddleia, which is quite exotic. Buddleia comes from China originally but it will live in virtually every environment, particularly in rough waste-land, and will colonise very easily. It's an exotic plant that actually does support British wildlife, because butterflies like it, unlike some escapees or non-native plants like the rhododendron, which is particularly useless for wildlife, and out-competes British trees and heathland plants.

I find most lawns that I see rather boring, they're just a green square, they don't really do anything for me at all. It's fine having that on a bowling green, there's a good reason for it, but do you really need it in your front garden, when you are so scared of it you can't even walk on it? Why not do something interesting with it and break it up a bit, stick some interesting shrubs in it, let the grass grow long in one corner, put in something unusual like a 'loggery'.

I have a couple of chickens at the end of the garden, and of course you don't need a cockerel, because the chickens don't need one to produce eggs. It's one way of knowing that your eggs are

Dandelion

'I mean, what is a weed? It's just a plant growing in the wrong place at the wrong time. If you had a potato growing in a rose garden it would be a weed, if you had a rose growing in a potato patch it would be a weed. It's a meaningless term, weed, there's no such thing as a weed really.'
Ray Harrington-Vail

Above: St Leonard's Hill. Story on page 94.
Below left and right: The Harris Garden at the
University of Reading. Story on page 77.

The pond create
Primary School,

Tucked away to one side of Knowl Hill CE Primary School is a small garden, an unexpectedly peaceful spot where it's easy to forget traffic going by a few hundred yards away on the busy Bath Road and the sound of children's voices in the playground.

In this small oasis, children can sit quietly enjoying the flowers, or can study the wildlife in the pond. 'Puggles Puddle', as the garden is called, was created in memory of a pupil, Mark Edward 'Puggles' Pugsley, who died in a road accident on June 10, 1983.

The garden was opened the following year for the enjoyment of children and teachers.

Above: The pond at Kennel Lane School.

Right: St Teresa's RC Primary School's chequerboad garden. Story on page 151.

an old swimming pool at Park Lane
rst. Story on page 114.

The sensory garden at Kennel Lane School. Story on page 92.

Above: Class One at Grazeley Parochial Primary School
planting lavender in their Victorian garden. Story on page 71.

Sylvia's Garden, at Newbold College, Binfield, created in 1912, which is now being restored. Story on page 100.

fresh, and you can partly feed them your waste food. You do have to be a bit careful not to give them anything that might give them salmonella, though. Many people during the Second World War, when food was short, used to keep a couple of rabbits or a couple of chickens in a glorified rabbit hutch. They don't require a lot of space and they are no more of a health hazard than a guinea-pig. Chickens will eat any insects and I deliberately throw snails and slugs into their run. Whatever's left – including their muck – goes into the compost bin. Composting is a very good way of recycling your garden and household waste. There are a number of commercial bins available if you've got a small garden – if you've got a big garden you can make a nice structure out of old pallets, or something similar – and you can turn waste into high quality compost. The depth of soil in the garden in the four years I have lived here has increased by about 6 ins, just by composting all our food waste and chicken manure.

People throw away grass cuttings, but they are a wonderful source of nutrients. They should be putting them around their shrubs and trees and runner beans. In a way they are throwing away a really good source of compost. Even though they can't use it immediately, they can put it in a rubbish sack in a sunny position, and in about three months they have got a really good compost. Even in a small garden, if you want just to grow a few herbs then you can use your grass cuttings. Where I work, quite a few local residents go for a walk in the morning and take their bag of grass cuttings and dump it in one of the council bins! They are throwing away something that they could use.

I decided a couple of years ago that I would like to do something special with the front garden because it is quite small. I had thought of creating a bog garden, putting flag iris and other bog-loving plants within a plastic sheet which is buried and filled up with soil. The plastic holds the moisture in – you just chuck a few buckets of water over it every day. However, I decided not to do that in the end,

INVALUABLE ADVICE

● Sow each seed as if it was the only one you have.
● Care for each plant as if it was your baby and as delicate.
● Sharpen your hoe and use it often.
● Don't believe anything anyone tells you until you've proved it for yourself.
Bob Flowerdew

Rosemary

because you do have to make certain you put water in every day, and it's in a very sunny position. I've always quite liked cottage gardens, because they give the appearance of being wild, but are, in fact, quite 'managed'. You sow things and plant things to give height at the back, and low things at the front, so my front garden is almost a cottage garden, just by the way things are planted. One of Geoff Hamilton's big things was a cottage garden where you grow your vegetables in with your flowering plants. You confuse the species by planting a couple of cauliflowers in with your flowering plants, then the cabbage white butterflies can't see or smell them, and therefore leave them alone. It's the same with carrot fly and carrots. If you plant carrots in the midst of scented plants, the carrot fly can't sense the carrots. There's a lot of logic in 'companion planting'. In the old-fashioned cottage garden, that is what they would do – a big mish-mash of different plants and a whole array of colour, and some of that colour would actually be from the vegetables.

I'm going to use some of Geoff Hamilton's ideas, together with what's there already, and come up with a pattern, draw it out on graph paper and play around with it a bit. I will be planting wallflowers, a tomato plant, maybe a potato, to give the colour and look of the the cottage garden. I won't actually eat any of the tomatoes if I get any from the front garden – too much benzine and lead!

Whether I will do this the next year depends on how well it works the first year. Part of the problem of course is time – if you're working you don't have the time to do all the management you'd need for some of the concepts you see on television. You have to compromise, and end up with something that maybe needs half an hour or less a week to pull out some of the more competitive weeds. If you're not careful, you just finish up with dandelions and nothing else. Two dandelions can look quite attractive, but when you get hundreds of them it gets a bit boring!

Romilly Swann

'My concept in gardening is to give some space for wildlife. We humans grab too much! **Ray Harrington-Vail"**

j *for jam line*

Blackberries on the branch line

The biggest and best blackberries to be found in Berkshire grow wild along the sides of an old railway line in the centre of Reading. They are a throwback to the days when the 'jam trains' chugged down the rails to the Co-operative Wholesale Society's jam factory.

The branch line, which was opened in 1908 to serve the central goods depot connecting it with various private sidings, including Bear Wharf, closed in 1983 and now provides a very pleasant walkway across the water meadows from Rose Kiln Lane to the main line at Southcote.

But the jam train has left its mark.

Along the embankments grow many soft fruits, including strawberries and raspberries, and an abundance of outsize blackberries, which have all sprung from the seeds of fruit scattered from the trains.

The best of these grow around the remains of the factory sidings near the Kennet, at Berkeley Avenue. These surely will not be allowed to remain long, before development smothers this little piece of the past for good.

In the meantime, here's the Swann family's tried and tested recipe for blackberry beer.

FORTNIGHT BLACKBERRY BEER
(for five gallons of beer)

> 1 bucket of blackberries
> 3 kg sugar
> 1 sachet of beer yeast (wine yeast will do)
> sterilised 5-gallon fermenting bin, large pan, potato masher, sterilised syphon tube, sterilised pressure barrel or bottles, wine bag or pillow case

Dissolve a tablespoon of sugar with the yeast in half a pint of lukewarm water and leave to froth up. In a large pan, mash the blackberries with a little water, whilst heating to boiling. Strain through wine bag or pillow case. Reheat liquid with more water to add sugar, heat till sterile (boiling) till sugar is completely dissolved.

Put the blackberry syrup into a five-gallon fermenting bin and fill with cold water to the mark. Finally stir in the yeast mixture, cover and leave for seven days.

Syphon into a pressure barrel or bottles to leave for another week.
Enjoy!

_k_ _for kennel lane school_

The Sensory Garden

The Sensory Garden was built two years ago. It was built where the old swimming pool used to be. We used to play on the concrete and remember the stinging nettles that grew near the edge. The concrete wasn't very nice because it was rough and bumpy. In the winter the concrete was icy, so it wasn't safe for children to play on.

The staff and students decided it would be nice to have a special garden for everybody at Kennel Lane School to use. We had to ask lots of people to help and we needed a lot of money to pay for the bricks and flowers and chairs to sit on.

Getting the ground ready

My class had to do a lot of digging with our teacher. We had to pull out all the weeds, it was very hard, sometimes it was very muddy. After that I got a rake and put manure in the soil. I remember the day when the men put the tarmac on top of the concrete. It was soft at first and smelt horrible. Then some men built the flower beds from bricks. We got some bricks and put them in a wheelbarrow, we took them in the Sensory Garden, we were helping the builders.

We had to dig a lot of holes. We took a plant out of its pot, we put it in the hole and gave it some water. We had to put the small plants at the front and the big plants at the back. We had to look at the plans to see where to put the plants. There were lots of plants and climbing plants and trees in the garden. The butterflies like some of

KENNEL LANE SCHOOL, in Bracknell, caters for pupils with a multiplicity of learning difficulties from an area ranging from Arborfield to Ascot, and from ages ranging from two to 19. Two years ago the school created a sensory garden and some pupils explain how it was made and what they feel about it

The lion's head water fountain

92

the flowers and there is a good smell of herbs, like perfume. We can hear the bees buzzing and the birds singing. Some of the leaves are soft and feathery and some are like leather.

There is a pond in the Sensory Garden. There are no fish in the pond at the moment. Volunteers put up a fence, they made a path and planted tall plants in the pond. In the spring there is frog-spawn in the water, later tadpoles come and they turn into frogs. Next to the pond is a greenhouse.

The Time Capsule

We helped bury the time capsule. We put the time capsule under the earth. The time capsule was buried under the ground with wood chippings on top. The capsule was buried in May 1996. In 24 years time the capsule will be opened in May 2020. In the capsule there is some writing and pictures about our school.

The Water Fountain

A group of us from my class helped put the large pebbles over the tank. We filled the tank with water. The fountain was finished. There is a lion's head on the wall above the pebbles. The water comes out from the lion's mouth, the water hits the pebbles. Sometimes the children put their hands in to see how cold it is. The water is very cold. The water sounds like a trickling sound.

Future plans

We would like a wild-flower area to plant some bulbs like bluebells and wild daffodils. We would like buttercups, daisies and poppies growing in the ground. We want some more plants for the flower beds and some climbing plants for the trellis. We hope to plant some more apple trees. In the Sensory Garden we would like to hear different sounds. We would like to get some windchimes.We hope to get a large rock to touch. It would be nice to have a bird bath.

WHAT WE LIKE ABOUT THE GARDEN

Michael: I like the Autumn time when the leaves fall down.

Steven: I like the lion's head, the water goes through. It is beautiful.

Mark: I like the summer-house. It will be good for the children in wheelchairs if they get cold.

Lyndsey: I like the pond.

Russell: I like the lion, it spits out water.

Marc: The trees in the garden are nice.

Stuart: The water sounds are nice.

Nick: It is excellent.

l *for st leonard's hill*

The lost gardens

"Full of charm as are the associations of the place with Horace Walpole's fascinating niece and the particular interest attaching to the work of Thomas Sandby, it is because St Leonard's Hill is a piece of Royal Windsor and yields the noblest view of the Castle from its eastern lawn that it remains one of the best-loved spots in Berkshire. It touches almost as intimately those traditions of spiritual beauty which remain nonetheless real in essence for being shadowy and elusive."

This quotation is taken from the sale catalogue of the St Leonard's Hill Estate in 1920. We can expect such a sale document to indulge in more than a little exaggeration, but the truth of the beauty and atmosphere of the Hill is repeated by other authorities.

St Leonard's Hill takes its name from the Chapel of St Leonard which is mentioned in 1215 as being in Losfield in the Manor of Clewer. During the medieval period pilgrims flocked to visit the Hermit and be absolved from their sins. Although we find a record in the Vatican archives of 1335, a silence descends on the scene during the catastrophe of the Great Plague between 1348 and 1368. As the numbers of pilgrims declined, the chapel probably fell into disrepair.

We find the next mention of the Hill in the letters of the Countess of Hertford who bought an old house near the site in 1737 and wrote how she "loved the situation… there is something in the retiredness… and the beautiful prospect from it". That prospect is

The matchless location of St Leonard's Hill in Windsor, which overlooks five counties, has entranced the rich, the royal and the famous over the centuries. It was the site of a medieval chapel, hermitage and holy well, and a place of pilgrimage. Modern-day pilgrims now flock to the entertainment park on the site. SHEILA ROONEY tells the story of this historic estate and mourns the passing of its fabulous gardens

part of the enduring beauty of St Leonard's Hill commanding as it does a view of five counties.

Maria Waldegrave, a beauty in her own right and illegitimate daughter of Sir Edward Walpole, is next upon the scene. When she was left a young widow on the death of her husband, Earl Waldegrave, the Duke of Gloucester fell under her spell and secretly married her in 1766. He bought St Leonard's Hill, extended it and set about transforming the gardens with the help of Thomas Sandby, one of the brothers famous for their construction of the water gardens of Virginia Water. A contemporary guidebook described the estate as 'a noble edifice commanding a most extensive and delightful prospect of the Thames'. The Duke and Duchess, having failed to be accepted at the court of George III, left for the continent where they could live more cheaply and be recognised as royalty. During their absence the estate was left to Henry Grenville who, in the fashion of the time, built a temple and a grotto in the grounds. Unfortunately we have no records to show what they looked like.

A reduced parkland of 75 acres was purchased by William, third Earl Harcourt. He died without an heir and after the death of his widow, the estate was occupied by La Marquisa Sophia d'Harcourt, widow of General Amédée d'Harcourt. Her diary expresses her feelings about the place: 'My dear sister consented to come with me that I might feel less melancholy... after a few days we came to St Leonard's Hill which far exceeded anything she had imagined of its beauty".

Back in the fifteenth century we find a mention of St Leonard's Hill in Malory's poem, Le Morte d'Arthur, *which tells the story of how Sir Launcelot, training for a tournament, stayed with the hermit of St Leonard's and went daily to the neighbouring spring where:*
'... he would lye down and see the welle sprynge and burbyl, and slept there.'

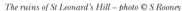
The ruins of St Leonard's Hill – photo © S Rooney

Many royal visitors came to the estate including Queen Victoria who loved to be driven there to look out over Castle Peep, a view made memorable by Victorian photographer, Bedford Lemere.

By 1869 the estate was sold again and came into the possession of an industrialist, Francis Tress Barry, who had made a fortune in the Portuguese copper mining business. He was looking for a country estate with parkland and a mature landscape. St Leonard's Hill was one of the best money could buy, with a peerless view of Windsor Castle. Money was lavished on both the house and gardens. Described as the Pleasure Gardens, the land was laid out as a plateau of lawn with charming maze-like walks and dotted with summer-houses.

Sir Francis Tress Barry assisted by his talented gardeners was the first man in England to grow the camellia successfully outside in the open and he planted them all over the estate without any wind protection. His blooms were exhibited at the Royal Horticultural shows in London and he won many medals and prizes. A lovely white bloom which he named after Lady Barry still blooms to this day.

The cultivation of camellias was continued by Reg Try, who bought the top of the Hill at the start of the Second World War. He found that all the beautiful mature trees, including Scots pines, sycamores, beech and chestnuts, had been compulsorily purchased for war purposes and one hundred and twenty three were felled. The Ministry of Defence then requisitioned the land as a training ground for the Grenadier Guards but Reg Try was able to exclude the soldiers from the kitchen garden and orchard.

The lost gardens of St Leonard's Hill are still there; the beautiful camellias struggling to bloom between the brambles, and the evergreens clothing the derelict colonnade. Even the plateau of the lawn is still recognisable beneath the shade of the majestic trees. The land has returned to nature but still retains what the ancient tribe of Atrebates recognised: that secret magic of the 'sacred grove'.

During the Edwardian period, the association of St Leonard's Hill with royalty continued as Edward VII attended house parties there during Ascot racing week. The delicate youngest son of Queen Mary, Prince John, was brought to St Leonard's Hill to be wheeled round the lovely gardens by his nurse. After the First World War, there were no staff to tend the grounds and most of the estate was sold off for housing.

The full story of St Leonard's Hill is told in *St Leonard's Hill: House, Hermitage and Hill* by Sheila and Pat Rooney (Published 1992.)

m for maidenhead

Margaret's little kingdom

When I first saw Herewards it was a big, old country house and the garden stretched right down to Lassell Gardens. My uncle got the job of gardener at the house and my aunt helped in the garden as well. I'd lived with my aunt and uncle since I was a baby and I used to play in the garden at Herewards during the summer holidays and weekends. I grew up in that garden. I can remember climbing into the pram when I was about three or four and lying under the quince tree. The aeroplanes sounded like big bumblebees, and I would look up into the quince tree and think, 'I won't go to sleep'. I'd look and I'd look but then I'd drift off. I love gardens, they're so calming. I'd like to be buried in the garden.

I remember at Herewards there was a high wall – it could have been 8ft or more – all round the garden. The house had a large conservatory and beyond that there was an area as big as my whole garden is today just for bantams and guinea-fowl. Their eggs were used for the house. There was a walkway down by the side of the pen with cobnut trees or bushes on the left-hand side. When you got beyond the guinea-fowl pen there was an archway in a wall and as you came through the archway, on both sides were big areas of narcissi and daffodils. You could pick a huge bunch and there were still hundreds left.

As far as I can remember there were four large greenhouses. One grew melons and in the other three there were tomatoes – yellow

MARGARET HNATIUK's secret garden has vanished now. She first discovered it about 50 years ago when she was a child. It was the garden of a large house called Herewards in Ray Park Avenue, Maidenhead, owned by a Mr Slattery. Margaret lived with her aunt and uncle, Mr and Mrs Sheldrake, who worked at Herewards as gardeners, next door to the house in which she now lives in Summerleaze Road

ones and red ones. In each one there was a salt and pepper pot so you could pick and eat the tomatoes. That was my favourite pastime.

There was a pathway that went right down the centre of the whole garden with archways along it covered with roses. On each side of the path were low box hedges. When I smell a box hedge now I think of the garden. Little paths branched off from the central pathway and one of them I called the Polyanthus Walk because on each side were masses of polyanthus, 2 ft or 3 ft deep.

On one side of the polyanthus we had a whole row of raspberry canes and also red-currant bushes, and on the other side there were vegetables, the sort of vegetables you wouldn't normally grow like asparagus and celery. I hardly ever tasted them. These were all grown for the big house. Just one man lived there. His name was Slattery and he was something to do with Threadneedle Street. Being young I didn't really take too much notice.

We grew fruit too. There were strawberry beds and in the walled garden, on the south wall, they grew peaches, apricots, figs and pears. I can remember the pears. I've never before or since tasted pears like them. I don't know what kind they were but they were huge and delicious. There were blackberries there and my uncle planted the late potatoes along the south wall because that was the warmest part in the autumn.

Down in the bottom half of the garden was the orchard full of fruit trees, cooking apples, eating apples of all denominations – Russets, Blenheims, everything, and then right at the bottom was a gateway in the wall that led out to a little bit of rough ground with a small footpath that only a few people had trodden leading out into. Lassell Gardens. That was my little kingdom. I called it the secret garden because there were lots of places to hide and I knew every inch of it. I was on my own, there were no other children, but I was never lonely. I always looked

'For years I dreamed about a garden and it was no garden I had ever seen – it wasn't Herewards. But I don't dream about it any more.'
Margaret Hnatiuk

Herewards as it is today

for flower fairies but the closest I got was finding a damsel fly. I've spent my life looking for fairies.

My uncle and aunt worked all day in the garden and it was a long day. I remember my uncle used to make his own compost. He had a big box with a roof on it and all the grass cuttings and any sort of rubbish went into it. Because you couldn't get a hosepipe long enough to come from the house to the garden, there were large square water-containers like troughs. I think my uncle pumped the water from the ground into the troughs and then used to fill the watering cans from them.

I spent the holidays in the garden which I enjoyed. I helped with the potatoes and I picked red-currants, white-currants, raspberries and blackberries. My aunt used to make jams and jellies and things like that – I think she used to do some cooking for Mr Slattery. We had to bring a lot of the lovely fruit and vegetables home. I used to go straight to the garden from school and help take the stuff home, walking up Ray Park Avenue with my doll's pram full of fruit and vegetables – and doll's prams in those days were bigger than baby's prams are today. I still only like home-grown vegetables.Some of the fruit and vegetables from the big house were sold but the flowers never were. There'd be vases of beautiful flowers in the house, wonderful. Now when I look back I think that, although I didn't know it then, I must have always loved flowers. When I smell sweet peas, I still think of the sweet peas my uncle grew in Summerleaze Road. He also used to grow prize chrysanthemums – they were enormous. Mr. Slattery used to exhibit some of them at the Chelsea Flower Show.

I was in my teens when I last saw the garden. I went away to Canada and when I came back years later they had built flats on the garden. I found it quite devastating. The house was still there – I think it was turned into a guest house and now it's a residential home – but that beautiful garden had gone.

'My daughter says to me, 'You smoke and you've got false teeth, you can't have any taste.' But I can tell the difference between a shop vegetable and a home-grown one. I have a teaspoon of shop veg but a whole plateful of my own – now they are grown by my husband.'
Margaret Hnatiuk

m *for moor close*

Sylvia's Garden

When the millionaire Charles Birch Crisp learned that he was to become a father again he could afford to make a grand gesture. The birth of this child of his middle age would be commemorated in style. The result was Sylvia's Garden, a beautiful Italian garden, with graceful flights of steps, pools, lawns, a pergola and gazebos. To create this garden Crisp turned to the young architect Oliver Hill who had already designed the superb gardens of his home, Moor Close, in Binfield, and transformed the house inside and out. Hill was only 25 when he drew up his plan for Sylvia's Garden in 1912, which makes the achievement the more remarkable.

Crisp had bought Moor Close, which was built in 1865, in 1906 and as he prospered he wished for a home to reflect his fortune. He had invested his money so successfully that by 1912 he was able to arrange a large loan for the Chinese government against Foreign Office wishes. He chose the unknown Oliver Hill to enlarge his house and in 1910 the young architect started on his first commission. Moor Close and its gardens reflect Hill's two great influences, the architect Sir Edwin Lutyens and the gardener Gertrude Jekyll. Hill designed the gardens with as much care and attention to detail as the house, believing that the grounds were an extension of the living space.

He created great formal shrub-gardens, lawns, ponds and terraces and employed 24 garden staff to care for them. Sylvia's Garden was

For more than half a century a beautiful Italian garden created to celebrate the birth of a millionaire's daughter in the grounds of Moor Close, Binfield, had been falling into decay. Now part of the grounds of Newbold College, owned by the Seventh-day Adventist Church, the garden is slowly and lovingly being restored. DR HARRY LEONARD, head of the humanities department at the college and a passionate gardener, is chairman of the Sylvia's Garden Restoration Committee the small jewel in the crown, a garden both romantic and classical, in which Hill's subtle use of different levels and numerous flights of steps created unexpected vistas everywhere. The original plan, still in the RIBA Library, and contemporary photographs reveal the full glory of the garden.

The garden was approached from the house by a balustraded bridge across a stream. Steps led to a court with a tile-on-edge pattern (a distinctive feature of the gardens) edged by Portland stone and pebbles, and two small lawns. Down another flight of steps was an oblong lawn surrounded by York stone paving and flower beds. The most dramatic feature of the garden is an imposing raised pergola, originally with a white marble floor, with gazebos at each end. An upper pool lies beyond the pergola, and another large lily pond with a fountain in it lies at the heart of Sylvia's Garden. Beyond it is a semi-circular platform from which, looking back, one has a superb view of Moor Close with flights of steps drawing the gaze up to the house, rising amongst the trees.

It is still possible to see how beautiful the garden must have been when Sylvia was growing up and famous visitors like the Prince of Wales (later Edward VIII), prime ministers Asquith and Lloyd George and the opera singer Dame Nellie Melba stayed in the house, but there is still a great deal of work to be done to counteract years of neglect and decay. The days of glory were all too brief for Charles Crisp, and by the late 1920s his fortunes had began to decline. The depression finished him. He was declared bankrupt in 1937 but long before that he had moved, ignominiously, to a lodge in the grounds where he spent

The classic beauty of Sylvia's Garden is being restored

his time trying to sell Moor Close, until his creditors foreclosed on him. After 1927 he had no money to spend on the grounds. The shrub gardens were neglected and Sylvia's Garden fell slowly into ruin. The house was bought by International Stores before Newbold College purchased the property in 1945.

However the cost of reclamation was beyond the college budget, and it was not until the late 1980s that the campaign to restore Sylvia's Garden began in earnest. By now vandalism as well as natural decay had ravaged the garden. Classical statues 'disappeared' and the dedicatory plaque was removed by an American student. Steps were broken, the pergola beams rotted, the gazebo roofs had fallen in, York stone paths and steps disappeared, and statues lay broken.

It was then that the Newbold Old Students Association stepped in and decided to raise funds for the restoration of the garden. Famous garden restorer, Paul Edwards, gave freely of his time in the early stages. English Heritage became interested and gave a grant to Elise Percifull, a horticultural student at the University of Reading, to draw up a programme of restoration and maintenance of the gardens and associated woodland. Grants have also come from Berkshire County Council, Bracknell Forest District Council, and Binfield Parish Council, but the majority of funding has come from old students. The restoration committee, enthusiastically led by Dr Harry Leonard, who is deeply committed to the project, has already done a great deal of work. Unsafe features – the gazebos' roofs, the pergola and the steps – have been restored, as has the central lily pond with its surrounding steps and borders. Students old and new have donated plants, benches and a sundial.

A year or two ago Sylvia's daughter visited the garden. It must have been a poignant moment seeing this once grand memento of her mother's birth. But the work goes on – a true labour of love – and gradually the garden is emerging from wilderness.

We no where Art do so triumphant see,
As when it Grafs or Buds the Tree:
In other things we count it to excell,
If it a Docile Schollar can appear
To Nature, and but imitate her well;
It over-rules, and is her Master here.
It imitates her Makers Power Divine,
And changes her sometimes, and sometimes does refine:
It does, like Grace, the Fallen Tree restore
To its blest state of Paradise before:
Who would not joy to see his conquering hand
Ore all the Vegetable World command?

Abraham Cowley
from The Garden

𝕟 *for newbury*

Dr Hickman's supreme sacrifice

About half-way along Market Street where it joined Bartholomew Street there was a very long wall, and behind it was a house. It fascinated me, this big old house on the corner. It was rather a gaunt-looking house, built in about the mid-1840s, and in the house lived a doctor. To me he was ancient. His name was Richard Hickman, quite a remarkable man, who was the coroner for Newbury. I used to see this big house and I wondered what was behind the wall, so one day I climbed up on my brother's back and looked over. I can still see that garden, almost as if I was looking at a photograph. It fascinated me. There were these long rows of wire with timber supports and plants growing horizontally along them – they were apples trained on espaliers I realised afterwards. At one end was a huge lean-to greenhouse, and the garden came down parallel and it terminated in the apex of a triangle.

There used to be a boy working for the doctor, running errands, helping the gardener, taking the weeds out of the gravel paths, sweeping up the leaves, chopping the wood in the old stables. It so happened the boy who had been doing the work had to give it up and I got the job. I was 11 years old. It necessitated going in for perhaps half an hour or three-quarters of an hour after school and on Saturday mornings I worked from nine o'clock to half past 12. This was all for the princely sum of three shillings. In 1929 that *was* quite a princely sum because boys who were apprentices were only

GERALD BRAFORD

*In 1929, as a boy of 11,
GERALD BRADFORD became
fascinated by a garden in
the centre of Newbury*

getting five shillings a week, and a bricklayer was lucky to get more than £3 a week. The money helped at home because my father was out of work a lot – he had been disabled in the First World War.

When I got the job, I became very interested in this garden and I learned lots of things. There were apples on those trees, mostly restricted forms – bush apples, pyramid, espalier or on cordons. Some of the fruit had a flavour I've never tasted today, not even the old varieties that I grow. One in particular I remember tasted just like honey.

The old doctor used to wear a white housecoat and he would push his glasses up above his eyes. His servants all came from the same family. The oldest lady, Mrs Kidd, was a very keen member of the Salvation Army. She didn't work for them full-time, but she came in and helped. Her elder daughter, Ena Kidd, was the housekeeper and her younger daughter, Alice, was the general maid. Alice was a Salvationist too, very devoted. They helped the poor and old of Newbury, making puddings and taking round bundles of firewood.

I remember, when I first went there, the housekeeper said, "Now, Gerald, the doctor's going down to the greenhouse. You must never go in that greenhouse." The greenhouse was whitewashed to keep out the excessive rays of the sun and inside it was the most wonderful vine of black grapes.

One day Dr Hickman went down to the greenhouse with a big pair of scissors and a trug and I thought, 'I must look in there'. In the summer, the door and the fanlight were often open and I just stood and looked and I was flabbergasted. That beautiful vine was almost like a tree of life. It had a short stem and grew out sideways and had the most luscious, beautiful, big, black grapes. They had a film on them. I remember some of the high-class fruit shops in Newbury had these wonderful grapes lying in a basket almost like

Romilly Swann

prize exhibits but they never had that film on them.

As Dr Hickman went into the greenhouse with his scissors I thought I'd see what happened. He put his glasses down over his eyes and went around and tenderly touched each bunch of grapes, inspected them, looked at them, stood back, gently touched them again, lifting them with the palm of his hand. I thought, 'What's he doing?' He'd go to each bunch of grapes and he'd stand back and survey them all like his children. He nurtured those grapes.

They wanted grapes for tea, I understood afterwards, and he'd gone to pick some. Suddenly he went up to one, looked at it, went back to another, and finally make a supreme choice – I always called it the supreme sacrifice. He took the bunch, held it lovingly under his left hand, nestled the grapes in his palm and gently cut them at the right place on the stem. He'd hold them with the end of the stem in the air and he looked at them and examined them. I could see in his face pride, satisfaction and joy.

It is a certain great joy that I experienced myself as a child growing up in the countryside, looking deeply into the centre of a primrose in the spring, and smelling the bluebells.

That was my first introduction to a real garden. That was Dr Hickman's garden. He died, and during the war it was taken over by the military. But now it's all gone, it's just a multi-storey car park.

Romilly Swann

NATURE AND THE NATURAL BALANCE

Gardens are for relaxation, so easing up, hanging on and taking time all help to make you a wiser gardener. New gardeners tend to rush in and make changes. It is always better to take stock, give a garden time to show itself, and gain a true measure of the positive assets and the problems.
Work with nature, not against it. A healthy natural balance between pests and predators, room for slow, soil-building decay, and a celebration of the changing seasons all help to make gardens far more interesting, and far more fun to manage. Fit in a pond if you possibly can, and try to find at least one corner where the weeds can grow, and the leaf-sweepings and rotting logs can boost the wildlife habitat.
Chris Baines

O *for offshoots*

Working with plants

When the Offshoots project had to move from their first home on land owned by the Thames and Chiltern Trust, Tudor House, Tidmarsh, near Pangbourne, staff and service users were a bit apprehensive. But their new home on a former estate in Englefield has proved an ideal site "It's a bit off the beaten track and it's fairly quiet but there's plenty of space so it's very well suited to what we are doing," said Allan Meakin. "In fact it's much better than the previous site which was bounded on one side by the M4 and had a big pylon in one corner so that when it was wet or misty you used to get the crackle from it all the time. It's much more pleasant here!"

The site used to be a kitchen garden for the Englefield estate, it even had melon and pineapple houses; but like a lot of country gardens it fell into decline after the First World War claimed the lives of its workforce. Although the original gardens have disappeared much of the estate remains as it was. From the front of the garden centre, you can look out over the estate parklands and see deer wandering about. "It's a very peaceful site, ideal for the people who come with particular difficulties," said Allan.

One of the objectives of the project is to move people from working in the sheltered, supervised environment of the Nursery into the world of 'real' work, not necessarily horticultural. The idea is to help the learning-disabled develop the skills they need to work in an ordinary environment such as time-keeping and social skills. Jeremy

Offshoots Nursery, at Englefield, near Theale, is the key element of a project aimed at providing work-related training for people with learning disabilities. In January 1995, Allan Meakin and Ron Hobbs set up the project up on behalf of the Thames and Chiltern Trust which commissions, manages and provides services for people with learning disabilities from long-stay mental hospitals in their move into residential accommodation in the community provided by the Trust. Most of the people who work at the Nursery come from these homes as GINA BOVAN discovered

Taylor, a staff member, believes that "helping to integrate the learning-disabled must be your goal or any effort you make in training people is half-hearted". Although some service users may never learn to work in an ordinary environment, others succeed.

On-the-job training plays a big role in helping service users achieve their potential. Allan says: "By doing horticulture in a workplace, service users learn lots of transferable skills. For example, in an ordinary work environment you do exactly what you're asked to do. One of the things we're concentrating on is to try to help them to adapt to doing things they don't necessarily like doing – and to find some fulfilment in doing that, by doing the job well. You may have a whole tray of plants to pot but once you've done that tray you can have a bit of a break."

The team consists of three horticulturalists, two support staff and four volunteers who work directly with the service users. Offshoots takes on people with very particular needs who require a lot of support while they are learning to do ordinary work. The project caters for a maximum of four people per day with learning disabilities. Service users can stay with the Nursery for as long as they like, until they decide they are ready to move on.

The five types of work within the Nursery are: nursery skills, site development, site maintenance, retail sales and garden maintenance. "People like particular sorts of work, some really like working with plants, and some really like the physical work like moving things, carrying bags of compost about and digging holes," said Allan. "We try to give people a choice about what they do here. For instance we always intended to do garden furniture, planters and benches.

Horticulture in the workplace

We've got one person who is very interested in that sort of work so he's busy making planters." Offshoots hopes to expand on these activities, along with taking on private gardening work.

Public response to the project has been very supportive, although initially customers of the old Englefield garden centre were not aware that it had closed down only to reopen as Offshoots. People have given gifts of money to help with the work of the project. Over time the Nursery will develop to become more like a garden centre customers are used to seeing, with a bigger range of goods. The way things are progressing, the project seems to be finding acceptance and support in the community.

Horticulture lies at the heart of achieving the aims of Offshoots Nursery. Open six days a week, it is committed to developing Englefield, and it is determined to become a commercial success in order to sustain its growth. Allan said: "We intend to be self-sufficient, so all the revenue that comes from plant sales will go towards the cost of the unit. We will be very competitive. We'll stand or fall on the quality of the plants we produce and the demand there is for them. We want people to come and buy our plants because they are good quality at reasonable prices but we do need the support of the general public. Come and support us, buy some plants!"

The work can be as satisfying for the helpers as the service users. Jeremy Taylor, a Reading University graduate in horticulture, said: "I started as a volunteer one day a week and then Allan needed more staff. I came in as a horticulturalist putting up polythene tunnels, clearing rubbish and sorting out hard-standing areas for displays and I train people as well. I've worked in nurseries before and been a bit frustrated by the monotony of it all, but here you are influencing people. A lot of these people would be stuck in day care centres not really doing a great deal. Here they have contact with the general public and we set down a routine for them which is what they need."

Michael is one of the learning-disabled who works at Offshoots He is not only learning about horticulture, he is also able to use his talents as an artist. His vivid number-plates adorn the building on the Offshoots site. He says: "I work here twice a week from 9am to 4pm. They are thinking of getting me a paid job here. I like it here because I do a lot of gardening. I help customers and carry stuff to their cars. I like plants a lot. They are colourful and pretty. The ones in the greenhouses, the rubber plants, have a different kind of texture – there's a dark green one and a light green one with a sort of yellowy colour. In my own garden, I grown my own chillis. My dad's Indian and likes raw chillis. And I like marrows. It's a good part of the week when I come here. It's job experience. They try and help me here. I like the people here."

O *for orchards*

An apple a day keeps the doctor away

In Britain the trend towards mass production of a limited range of apples is augmented by the mass eradication of our old traditional orchards which have been grubbed out at the rate of 50,000 acres a decade over the last 30 years. It need not be so. By freeing them from the economic imperative to create wealth we can regard them more as 'sacred groves' or common lands for relaxation, pleasuring and community events as well as providing an unpolluted habitat for wildlife to flourish in the hearts of our towns, cities and villages. The leap from concept to practical application in the creation of community orchards can be a bit of a struggle but it is relatively simple once land has been acquired.

The most pressing need for a successful community orchard project is the acquisition of land suitable for both planting with trees and access by people. This means that communities are in competition from the outset with other possible uses for such land which could be valuable as housing or industrial development land. A consultation with your local planning authority would be helpful at an early stage in the scheme so that the planning officer is aware of your ambitions and may be able to direct you towards developers who are keen to create an orchard as part of planning gain in a certain place. There are lots of potential pitfalls in the planning process so help from Rural Action or other community-based information services would aid your understanding of the legal issues.

There used to be 2,000 varieties of apples grown all over Britain but you will not notice many of them in the supermarkets. As the apples have gone, so have the traditional orchards which are disappearing at an alarming rate. We should be creating orchards not cutting them down, argues DUNCAN MACKAY, a co-founder of the New Road Cyderists and author of Apples, Berkshire, Cider, *and he explores the ways and means by which community orchards can be achieved and the benefits to be derived*

However, if you are successful and manage to acquire suitable land then you will need to consider a plan and a programme to make the community orchard take shape. In the first instance you will need an accurate survey of the property so that you know what you have and where everything is. This might need several seasons to achieve especially if you have an ecologically rich habitat. It would be best to seek the advice of your local naturalists' trust (such as BBONT) or a local authority ecologist who will be able to tell you if it is already listed as a Wildlife Heritage Site, a Site of Special Scientific Interest or has protected species using it. If there are no constraints then you can proceed to the preparation of a planting and management plan. Don't be put off by the terminology but use such a plan as a common-sense guide to what you intend to do, and think about the potential consequences before you do it.

Romilly Swann

A key input at this stage will be assistance from someone with experience of old orchards and tree spacing. Spacing is not an immediately obvious problem on bare land but in twenty or thirty years' time the distance between trees will have become a critical feature of your orchard management. Old orchards with low fertiliser inputs would need 40-ft spacings to allow proper growth and fruiting. This type of layout also gives plenty of space for other communal activities and could be the optimal distance for larger orchards. Avenues, edges or special features within the layout of the orchard might present other exciting possibilities where a helpful landscape architect could assist you achieve your ideas. Planning on paper is a vital part of the process and can save a lot of effort later.

The choice of trees to put onto your plan should also be fun and set a lot of ideas off. You can do collections of local fruit, alphabets of

I would plant an orchard, and have plenty of such fruit as ripen well in your country. My friend, Dr Madden, of Ireland, said, that, "in an orchard there should be enough to eat, enough to lay up, enough to be stolen, and enough to rot upon the ground."

Dr Johnson, April 18, 1783
Boswell' s Life Of Johnson

fruit names, groves associated with cultural themes or historical links. Don't forget the delicate hues of blossoms and the successive effect of spring fruit-buds bursting into flower. You may also need to plant native crab-apples for cross-pollination and it could be a good idea to use sloes, damsons, wild plums and greengages as colourful edible hedges or windbreaks and roosts for wild birds. Research your locality and see if there are any special associations with fruit or orchards.

Consider underplanting your orchard with wild-flowers and shallow-rooting native bulbs so that you can recreate the feel of an old meadow. Ensure that you obtain any such plants from a reputable supplier such as the Farming and Wildlife Advisory Group, Little Hidden Farm, Hungerford. Take care in your choices if you also intend to graze livestock such as sheep in due course. Ascertain how you want to manage and maintain your orchard to maximise both community use and wildlife interest. Welcome in 'weeds' such as docks as these are the natural food sources of the colourful but much maligned bullfinch and other seed-eating birds. Aim to achieve a natural balance between all members of the wildlife community and your orchard will become a hugely instructive outdoor classroom for the human community. Decide your policy on chemicals from the outset and seek the advice of specialists such as the Soil Association or the Henry Doubleday Research Association on organic orcharding and natural 'pest' control.

Obviously if the land you have obtained is already an orchard or part-orchard then only a few of the above suggestions will need working on. Former traditional farm orchards have been successfully translated into community orchards by just allowing people free access, subject to a few safeguards to protect the trees and the health of the land. Such places will still need some management planning to ensure a succession of trees to fill the gaps left as old ones die off. Incidentally, storm-blown trees often do not die but just start growing

BOOKS TO READ ABOUT APPLES AND ORCHARDS

Apples, Berkshire, Cider.
Hall, Hay and Mackay.
Two Rivers Press, 1996

Apple Map of Britain.
Common Ground

Berkshire Environmental Action Pack.
Babtie Group.
Berkshire County Council, 1995

Holding your Ground.
Common Ground.
Wildwood House, 1987

Local Distinctiveness.
Common Ground, 1993

Orchards: a guide to local conservation.
Common Ground, 1989

The Book of Apples.
Joan Morgan and Alison Richards.
Ebury Press, 1993

The History and Virtues of Cyder.
R K French.
Robert Hale, 1982

again from a recumbent position. Do not be persuaded that such trees need 'tidying up' as they add the unexpected to the scene and become great seats for children.

Getting stuck in to the job after all the planning stages and discussions can be attempted at any time of the year but trees should normally only be planted during the winter dormancy period. The best time to start people working is probably either the spring or summer preceding your tree planting efforts. The weather is usually kinder and it is easier to attract volunteers if you also have some sort of event such as a barbecue. Most bare land sites will need some degree of preparation and people will need directing. If you contact the British Trust for Conservation Volunteers (BTCV) they will be able, for a small membership fee, to show you the best ways of tackling the co-ordination of project volunteers and obtaining a supply of tools from

*'Cyder-making' drawn and etched by
William Henry Pyne in 1806*

their stores. Do not spray chemicals or use chainsaws unless you have the necessary training and certificates of competency. Take enormous care when lighting bonfires. Instruct older children and teenagers in the proper use of all sharp tools and do not allow anyone to use tools unless they have satisfactorily demonstrated their capability. Watch out for underground pipes (usually water but possibly gas or electricity) and overhead powerlines. Ask BTCV about insurance cover (just in case damage occurs accidentally) and appoint someone sensible or with Health and Safety experience to act as site supervisor. Always carry a good first aid kit and a mobile phone if you can. Always get a leader to describe the day's work programme before anybody begins a task. Do not become wise after the event! It might appear to be a daunting list just to plant a few apple trees but it is necessary and sensible until you have confidence that the project can effectively manage itself without potential hazard to people or property. BTCV regularly runs an imaginative series of training courses in all practical conservation matters.

Lots of people all over Britain are doing it and many more are trying to do it! 'Pippin Park' at Colnbrook, in Berkshire, is a small community orchard planted on land owned by the local authority and celebrates the life of Richard Cox. The world's most famous apple – the Cox's Orange Pippin – was developed in the village and specially commissioned seats in the shape of the letters COX commemorate the event. Apple trees here were planted by local primary school children co-ordinated by the Colne Valley Groundwork Trust and the campaigning group Common Ground. Volunteers – the Friends of Prospect Park – are planting an orchard on land owned by Reading Borough Council. Despite a setback caused by vandalism the group is persevering with its efforts and plans to plant a number of fruit trees.

In Waltham St Lawrence, a community orchard is being planned around a number of derelict allotment plots owned by the parish council and a Rural Action grant is being sought.

In Twyford and Ruscombe, the New Road Cyderists decided to aim high and applied for a Millennium Commission grant to buy and plant up to 50 acres of land as a community orchard. They successfully obtained the sanction of the Commission to proceed past the first stage but, unfortunately, none of the local landowners were prepared to sell the group any land and time has now run out. However, on the basis of the group's researches and aspirations it entered the prestigious Henry Ford European Conservation Awards and won first prize in the UK heritage projects section.

Once you have your orchard and your trees are producing fruit then apple activities will become a focus for people (as well as providing food for lots of other creatures). Why not create rights of 'pommage' and register your orchard as common land giving it added protection and providing local people with an individual householders' right to take fruit. Fruit eating is healthy and deliveries of apples could be made to those unable to collect their own. Schools, clubs and religious organisations could participate in harvest festivals, orchard blessings, wassailing, Hallowe'en events and blossom walks. Making something happen at every season of the year adds vitality to the orchard and brings in newcomers to the community. If you could get a small cider press or are lucky enough to be given the chance to restore an old one, you could make fresh apple juice or cider. The harvest is a great time for getting lots of people involved and sharing the bounty of the trees.

p *for park lane school*

From pool to pond

At Park Lane School, there used to be a swimming pool. No one could swim in there any more because the heater and the pipes were broken and the plastic liner was all ripped. The swimming pool was changed into a garden for the children to work in. Most of it was filled in, but some of it was turned into a pond.

Every week, on Thursday and Friday lunchtimes, some children called the 'Greenies' come and clear the garden up. We pull the blanketweed out of the pond and pull the weeds out of the flower beds.

The governors hired someone to dig some flower beds in the playground and trees were put into them. Then tubs were bought for both playground areas, and we planted shrubs in them.

In the summer there are lots of frogs, and the flowers brighten up the place. The school collects daffodil bulbs in the autumn to plant outside the front of the main building in our only bit of grass.

Sarah Windiate and Holly Sutherland (Y5)

Seeds and lolly sticks

Mr Brayshaw gave us each a seed and a lolly stick and we put our name on it. We went into the environmental area. Mr Brayshaw put some holes in the flower bed. We lined up and put our seed in a hole, one by one. Every day Miss Boardman got some people to

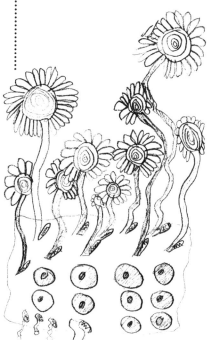

An old swimming pool became the inspiration for an environmental project at PARK LANE PRIMARY SCHOOL, in Tilehurst, Reading. Some of the children tell the story

water them. We waited a few weeks and some heads were popping out. Miss Boardman's was the first. After the six weeks of the summer holiday, most of the flower heads had come out and brightened the area up.

Jamie-Lee Tegg (Y5)

Our school garden

I have only just joined the green group but I am having a wonderful time. I have helped plant some trees down the field. We got quite dirty. It was great fun. Mr Evans has been a great help; he's shown me how to use the tools. Now I really like gardening. I like the garden a lot. I will miss it a lot when I leave this school. I hope my new school has a garden. I hope we have some more things to plant soon, as we have asked for any spare bulbs.

Steven Myles

THE TREES

In the field earlier this year, we planted some young trees. Mr Evans, a Year 6 teacher who is the leader of Green Group, the club that works in the garden at school, took some spades and forks down and we dug some holes for the trees to go in. The idea was that in thirty years or so, the trees will give shade or protection against the weather and be there as a memory.

Unfortunately, the foxes got half of the trees so it's fifty-fifty between us and the foxes

Edward Mayhew (Y6)

PRACTICAL TIPS

Painting the outside of terracotta pots and containers with natural yoghurt will encourage lichens. Surfaces will become well weathered in a year or two.

When buying bulbs, ensure that they have been grown for sale by responsible nursery men and not plundered from the wild.

If you use netting to cover fruit crops – particularly strawberries and raspberries – check regularly to ensure that birds have not become trapped or entangled.

Never dig up wild plants for your garden. In most cases it is illegal to do so – plus the fact that the plants rarely naturalise successfully in a 'foreign' habitat.

Try erecting two rows of beansticks so that the tops are further apart than the bottoms. This will allow more light to reach the plants than if they are grown in the traditional way.

𝑝 *for pineapple*

'A grateful acidity'

Tradition has it that the first pineapple grown in England was raised at Dorney Court by John Rose, gardener to Sir Philip Palmer, who owned the house from 1658 to 1683.

Sir Philip's half brother, Sir Roger Palmer, who became Earl of Castlemaine and was married to the King's mistress, was given the top of a 'Barbados Pine' by Charles II, which he brought to Dorney and handed to John Rose, who is mentioned in history and gardening books. So from small beginnings pineapples were produced.

The field where the pineapples were grown is near the Pineapple public house at Lake End, Dorney (just over the Berkshire border) and is still owned by the Palmer family. It is now called the Pin Garden and there was most likely a walled garden there in the 1660s. There were no greenhouses so John Rose dug deep trenches to protect his experiments against frost. When a sizeable fruit had been produced he was allowed to present it to Charles II in 1665. The king was very pleased and offered him a position as a royal gardener at Hampton Court, where he laid out some water gardens. So, Sir Philip lost his excellent gardener. John Rose probably did work for other employers and being such a clever horticulturalist he was bound to go up in the world.

John Rose, who was born in 1633, was acquainted with John Tradescant Junior, head gardener to Charles I, and Elias Ashmole

The pineapple first arrived in Great Britain in the 17th century, but quite when remains unclear. There is a local story that the first pineapple was grown on the Berkshire/Buckinghamshire border as LOIS PARKER describes

who founded the Ashmolean museum in Oxford with the Tradescants' collection of curios.

There is a sketch of the pineapple being presented to Charles II in Dorney Court taken from the original painting by Dankaerts which is in Ham House, but the house in the background is neither Dorney Court nor Ham House.

There is also a large model of a pineapple in the great hall at Dorney Court commemorating the event.

However, it is believed that a pineapple was grown earlier at Oatlands Park, an old palace in Walton-on-Thames, Surrey, where Queen Henrietta Maria had lived, before it was rased to the ground during the civil wars. Oliver Cromwell is said to have had the pineapple pits destroyed.

This accords with what John Evelyn, the diarist and garden lover, wrote on August 9, 1661:

"I first saw the famous Queen Pine brought from Barbadoes, and presented to his Majesty [Charles II]; but the first that were ever seen in England were those sent to Cromwell four years since."

However, he seems to have forgotten this sighting seven years later when he reported on August 19, 1668:

"Standing by his Majesty [King Charles II] at dinner in the presence, there was of that rare fruit called the King-pine, growing in Barbadoes and the West Indies; the first of them I have ever seen. His Majesty having cut it up, was pleased to give me a piece off his own plate to taste of; but, in my opinion, it falls short of those ravishing varieties of deliciousness described in Captain Ligon's History [*A True & Exact History of the Island of Barbados*, 1657], and others; but possibly it might, or certainly was, much impaired in coming so far; it has yet a grateful acidity, but tastes more like the quince and melon than of any other fruit he mentions."

Romilly Swann

p *for pub*

The Tardis garden

In the first year that Linda and Charles Tringali took over The Plough on the Green, in Newbury, their pub garden proved to be a constant source of surprise for them. The previous landlord had been there for 11 years, and the Tringalis had no idea what was planted there.

"Every time we went out there, something new was coming up," said Linda. Nevertheless, they rose to the challenge of maintaining what was obviously a well-kept garden, and in 1996 won a Best Pub Garden award.

The garden at The Plough is well-hidden, out to the side of a pub that is itself not entirely obvious to passers-by. The pub was built before the rest of the houses in Greenham Road, so stands back at an offset angle from the road. It was built to face the green, and would do now if it were not for housebuilders over the last hundred years or so who have built houses at a more regular angle, closer to the road. You could easily drive past, and if there were no pub sign hanging by the roadside, you might never notice that the pub was there.

Entering the gap between the houses, you see the little whitewashed pub with a weeping willow, an apple tree to one side, and tubs, pots and creepers decorating the front of the building. The task of watering all these pots has been made a little easier since a semi-automatic watering system was installed to save hanging out of a window or climbing up to the roof. Besides, with so much in the back

When The Plough on the Green pub in Newbury won a best garden award, many of the regulars were not even aware there was a garden. The pub's well-kept secret is discovered by JOHN DAVEY

garden to look after, you need a bit of help sometimes. However, before the Best Pub Garden plaque went up on the wall of the bar, many of the pub regulars never even realised that the pub had a garden, let alone one that was good enough to win a prize.

When you enter the low-ceilinged old pub and walk through to the back of the bar, if you peek through the side window, you can see a traditional red telephone box and, if you look a little beyond that, a small fountain and a barbecue area. However, you have to go past that and through a side gate to find the garden. It expands unexpectedly out beyond the narrow road frontage to both sides, and runs behind several of the houses between which it is sandwiched on the Greenham Road.

"It's a bit of a Tardis really," says Linda.

Just like the Tardis, the garden stretches out much further than you might expect, in all directions. There is a slide for the children tucked in one corner (though you would not notice it straight away), and wooden benches all around for eating and drinking outside. In the summer, many of the benches are shaded by the old apple trees, which Linda believes originally formed part of an orchard. The many bushes and shrubs are at each edge of the irregularly-shaped garden, and the lawn is punctuated by beds of all kinds of fuchsias, geraniums, and annuals. Linda tried growing nasturtiums last year, but they never really seemed to flourish in the flower beds. Not wanting to give them up entirely, she put them into tubs, where they burst into life, with big splashes of red, orange and gold. She likes to arrange the garden into colour themes – a red corner, an orange corner, and so on.

Having won the pub garden competition, Linda had plans for the following year. She bought plenty of seeds rather than buy everything ready from a nursery. The garden needed constant maintenance all through the winter, and the the milder days of early spring meant there was no let-up.

Romilly Swann

"With the weather getting warmer, we didn't have our day off this week because we were working in the garden," she said. "The geraniums that have overwintered in pots out of the way of the frost needed to be put out soon, and there were all those seeds to see to. The weekend barbecue season started in April, and we wanted the garden to look good."

With such a garden to look after, the Tringalis sometimes need a little help, especially with customers to serve, food to cook, and real ale to look after. When Charles was ill last year, and was unable to do lots of strenuous work in the garden, it helped that they had a couple of friends nearby who were willing to put their hand to the flower beds. Once a week, they have a gardener in to cut the lawn but all the planning, and most of the hard graft, is still down to them.

Romilly Swann

PICNICS AT PARK PLACE

One hundred years ago the place to go for an outing or picnic was the beautiful and unusual grounds of Park Place, at Remenham, whose hanging woods have been celebrated for two centuries.
Park Place stands high on a hill overlooking a long loop of the Thames, with Oxfordshire beyond. The grounds are full of interesting features: the 'Happy Valley' with its fake classical ruins, some cottages in Gothic style, and the top of a church steeple said to be from St Bride's in Fleet Street. There is also a bridge called General Conway's Bridge, built partly with stone brought by barge from the remains of Reading Abbey, and whose construction was supervised by the Revd Humphrey Gainsborough, brother of the painter.
More mysterious are the 40 large stones brought from Jersey in 1785 but according to John Betjeman and John Piper they once formed an ancient burial chamber.
Extensive lavender plantations were once a feature of the Wargrave side of the estate but little now remains of these.
In the latter part of the 19th century the owners allowed the Happy Valley and the lawn by the boathouse to be used for Sunday-school outings and picnic parties. Some of the visitors came to the landing-place near Conway's Bridge by horse-drawn barge.

Tony Barham

q *for queens and kings*

Grand gardens and royal retreats

The gardens of Windsor Castle, being subject to the whims of kings, queens and nature, have changed constantly over the centuries, though their different appearances have been far less well documented than those of the Castle itself.

For several hundred years, however, there was a constancy: on the warm south side, in what was called the 'Garden Plot', a vineyard flourished. It is first referred to in 1156, and in the time of King Richard II it was said that vines "grew in great plenty". Good wine was produced and even sold. As late as the reign of George III a small vineyard was cultivated directly under the Castle's southern walls. Now as the tourists climb up Castle Hill there's nothing to look at but grass.

On the other side of the Castle is the site of a garden that never was. In 1698 Sir Christopher Wren planned for William III "an elaborate vista of formal gardens with an ornamental canal and fountains to the river", on the piece of land known as 'Maestricht' following a spectacular re-enactment there in 1674 of the siege and capture of the city by the French. Advice for the garden was sought of the venerable André le Nôtre who created the canal at Versailles. But the King died, and although Queen Anne revived the plan and digging began the scheme was abandoned, possibly because of flooding: a depression in the ground which still fills at times of heavy rain is all that remains of grandiose intentions.

Much has been written about that most recognisable of royal homes, Windsor Castle, yet the history of its gardens is little known. HESTER DAVENPORT traces the changes that have taken place to the royal gardens over the centuries and tells the story of the famous gardens of Burford House, in Windsor, built by a king's mistress

CHARLES II

When, likewise in 1698, the indefatigable traveller and breathless recorder Celia Fiennes climbed the Round Tower, she looked over the top and saw that

"the town of Winsor looked very well, there were severall noblemens houses Duke St Albans and fine gardens; just by it is the Lord Guidolphins [Godolphin's] house and gardens, there I could see the fine walk [the Long Walk] or rather road planted with trees, of a huge length into the Forrest which King Charles [II] made for his going out in divertion of shooting …"

The Duke of St Albans was Charles II's son by Nell Gwyn (the title was reputedly awarded after Charles had reproved Nellie for addressing the child as "Bastard", to which she replied "What should I call him then?"). The King gave her land on the old royal Garden Plot where she built the splendid Burford House. Its gardens were renowned, and their later arrangement can be seen clearly on an engraving of 1708 by Jan Kip. It can also be seen that at that date the Long Walk did not run up to the Castle as it does today: it ended at the public road below Burford House which led to Old Windsor.

The other grand garden shown by Kip had belonged to Lord Godolphin, but by then his house had become part of Queen Anne's much-loved home. Celia Fiennes paid a second visit to Windsor a few years later and her description of the garden, though not quite fitting Kip's plan, gives us a verbal equivalent:

"you come on a terrass of gravell then descend stepps down a green banck to a large green space that has 4 bench seates painted white, behind them is a green bank and a large space of green on either end fill'd with trees – lawrells filleroy [phillyrea] cyprus yews, heads and pirramids, and mirtles; this is fenced with iron palasadoes painted, to another garden cut in squares and

What wondrous life is this I lead!
Ripe apples drop about my head;
The luscious clusters of the vine
Upon my mouth do crush their wine;
The nectarine and curious peach
Into my hands themselves do reach;
Stumbling on melons, as I pass,
Ensnared with flowers, I fall on grass.

Meanwhile the mind from pleasure less
Withdraws into its happiness;
The mind, that ocean where each kind
Does straight its own resemblance find;
Yet it creates, transcending these,
Far other worlds, and other seas;
Annihilating all that's made
To a green thought in a green shade.

Here at the fountain's sliding foot,
Or at some fruit-tree's mossy root,
Casting the body's vest aside,
My soul into the boughs does glide;
There, like a bird, it sits and signs,
Then whets and combs its silver wings,
And, till prepared for longer flight,
Waves in its plumes the various light.

Andrew Marvell
from Thoughts in a Garden

figures with all sorts of flowers and greens which has at the end a cut hedge and leads on to a sort of orchard with dwarfe trees; these gardens and orchards is in gravel walks and long green walks, in variety as such a thing in miniature can admitt."

The two famous gardens started to lose identity at the same time as the vineyard disappeared, during the reign of George III. Accommodation was needed for his huge family and Burford House was bought for the royal daughters, while Queen Anne's 'little box' was demolished and a barrack-like block, called Queen's Lodge, erected instead. Queen Charlotte was said to have regretted the loss of the gardens for what was left between the two was "more of a passage to both than a retreat into the fresh air; moreover every window looked into it". The lack of privacy was made worse by the public path to Datchet which ran under the Castle walls and overlooked the garden at the front.

Queen's Lodge was in turn demolished in George IV's radical transformation of the Castle. He was thus enabled to extend the

A view of Burford House, to the left of the picture, with its splendid gardens. Queen Anne's House is at the foot of Windsor Castle mound. Drawing by Olivia Davenport from the 1708 engraving by Kip

Long Walk, which now sweeps dramatically up to the George IV Gate. The rest of the once-admired gardens were covered by the Royal Mews – arguably a less happy exchange. In search of fresh air and privacy the King created a sunken garden below high walls along the East Terrace, and was presented by the King

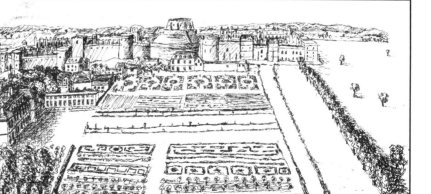

of France with thirty-four trees for an orangery. Citizens were able to witness "a floating forest" as the barge carrying them came up the Thames. But despite the walls shielding him from public gaze the King was conscious of the Castle windows looking down on him as he strolled, and he could not like his new garden.

It was Prince Albert who gave the royal family real privacy when he closed the old public highways and sanctioned new roads, one through 'Maestricht' to Datchet, the other to Old Windsor and Staines crossing the Long Walk much lower down, thus creating the royal estate as we know it today. The twentieth century has not seen much change to the gardens, apart from the landscaping of the beautiful Moat Garden below the Round Tower.

But one very small garden, designed by Gertrude Jekyll for Queen Mary, should be mentioned, so small that it can be stowed away in a drawer. In the garden of the Queen's Dolls' House nature has come to a stop: the roses never fade, the trees do not lose their leaves, and the perfect velvet lawn will never need cutting by the tiny lawn-mowers standing ready.

An 18th century gardener drawn by Olivia Davenport after paintings by Paul Sandby

'LAW AND FORM AND DUE PROPORTION'

Gardener:
Go, bind thou up yon dangling apricocks,
Which, like unruly children, make their sire
Stoop with oppression of their prodigal weight:
Give some supportance to the bending twigs. –
Go thou, and, like an executioner,
Cut off the heads of too-fast-growing sprays,
That look too lofty in our commonwealth:
All must be even in our government. –
You thus employ'd, I will go root away
The noisome weeds, that without profit suck
The soil's fertility from wholesome flowers.

Servant:
Why should we, in the compass of a pale,
Keep law and form and due proportion,
Showing, as in a model, our firm estate,
When our sea-walled garden, the whole land,
Is full of weeds; her fairest flowers choked up,
Her fruit-trees all unpruned, her hedges ruin'd,
Her knots disorder'd, and her wholesome herbs
Swarming with caterpillars?

William Shakespeare
King Richard II, Act III, Scene iv

r *for rainforest*

Tropical Berkshire

It is, of course, impossible to replicate the extraordinary complexity and vitality of the rainforest in Britain's climate. However, one of the best attempts is Wyldcourt rainforest conservation centre, at Hampstead Norreys. Here resides a well-established collection of tropical plants, including many rare, veteran specimens occupying three climate-controlled glasshouses.

Amazonica (semi light intensive, humid 18°C (65°F) min) – This is the largest house, named after the giant water-lily, Victo*ria amazonica*, an example of which flourishes in the pool. Around the pool clamours a myriad of ground-dwelling and epiphytic (tree-dwelling) plants, including some spectacular orchids and bromeliads, amongst lianas (climbers), shrubs and tree ferns. It offers a chance to see some of the flowers of the rainforest canopy rarely glimpsed from the forest floor, and to hear the sound of native rainforest birds.

Lowland tropical (very humid and warm 21°C (70°F) min) – This house is crammed with lush understorey plants, which have dark (chlorophyll rich) glossy leaves, designed to repel the growth of mosses and algae which would deny them precious sunlight. Their flowers, though often not brightly coloured, are amazing structures.

Cloud forest (cooler but still humid 10°C (50°F) min) – This house contains many epiphytes including wonderful orchids and bromeliads which thrive without soil in the misty foothills of tropical mountain ranges.

ROMILLY SWANN was fortunate enough to travel through the Amazon rainforest in 1994 to work as a botanical artist at a reserve called Ducké, near Manaus, in Brazil. Back home in Berkshire, the closest to the real thing is Wyldcourt rainforest conservation centre, at Hampstead Norreys

r *for ranikhet primary school*

My favourite garden

Jamie Hawkins: My garden has lots of plants in it. It has got trees and flowers. Next year we're going to plant some pumpkin seeds but the only problem is the rabbit and guinea pigs because they all fomp [sic] about.

Richard Glancy: My favourite garden is my garden because it has a wall to climb on and jump off and a little fence so I can talk to my neighbours.

Alicia Rampton: My favourite garden is my Nan's and Grandad's because it is really big. They live on a farm. The reason why I like it is because you can play anything you want to play. At the back of their house is a big square. In the big square there are lots and lots of flowers, plants and vegetables. They have got Brussels sprouts, swede, carrots, runner beans and cabbage. These are the flowers they have got: buttercups, dandelions and lots more. I wish I had a garden like that.

Liam Fairhurst: My best garden has big and small trees in. It is good for playing football. It is Michael's garden.

Michael Bosher: My favourite garden is Liam's garden because there is a bush in it. It has an unstable swing in it, quite a large garden too. The bush is good for playing in.

Samantha Pearcey: I imagine I had a garden. It has got smoke coming out of the grass, it has a seaside in it. There is a place where it has got ice and snow. There is a playground and there is a playhouse.

Gardens are not just for plants as children from RANIKHET PRIMARY SCHOOL, in Tilehurst, Reading, explained when they were asked to describe their favourite garden

Sheena Easton: Every day I go to my friend's house. We go in her garden. She has got a shed in her garden and she has a hutch because she had two rabbits, a male and a female. They had babies but the babies died and they had to get rid of the male. They had to get more plants because the rabbits ate them.

Jamie Froude: My aunty's garden has got lots of flowers in her back and front garden and she has lots of plants as well and she is planting some more in her front garden. My aunty's garden has got a five-a-side football pitch and she has got a big swimming pool as well. She has got a pond with lots of fish and she has got a big, long, long fish in her pond

Nicola Basden: I like to imagine that I had a fun house in my back garden and I would play in it all day, and I like to imagine that I had a swimming pool in my back garden and I would swim in it all day, and I like to imagine that I had a log flume in my back garden and I would play on it all day. It would be fun if I did have all the things. I would be happy.

Cassie Bray: Every day I go in my garden I have a smile on my face because I love my garden and every day I go in my back garden my dog and I always play. My dog likes the garden. Every day I water my plants and when we go out my dog likes to stay in the back garden.

Gemma Bryant: I like my garden because my favourite thing to do is give my brother a running race. I like riding my bike up and down the garden. I skip round and round the garden. I read books in the garden. I climb my tree at the bottom of my garden.

Sarah Pegler: I have a nice back and front garden. I have got one pet in my back garden, it is a rabbit, her name is Lucy. I have got skates. I put them on and I skate in the back garden. But Lucy does not get scared.

r *for roots*

Rooting out the problem

Years of work bent over a microscope studying the roots of trees and shrubs has not dimmed Ian Richardson's love of trees. "Every time I issue a report, I feel very sad and think, is that another tree cut down? But you have to strike a balance. Sometimes trees are in very silly places, especially when they are allowed to get too big. If you keep a tree small, it doesn't take up as much water because it hasn't got as many leaves on it, so you can afford to keep it in your garden."

Ian's business is concerned almost exclusively with the identification of pieces of tree root, grubbed up from underneath subsiding buildings, and sent by post from all over the country, mainly by insurance companies anxious to apportion blame for the causes of damage.

A PhD botanist with the training of a plant taxonomist, Ian has written books on plants from various regions of the world. Even more relevant to his future career was his time on the research staff of the Royal Botanic Gardens, Kew, where he worked in the plant anatomy laboratory identifying pieces of tree root. This research culminated in a book, written jointly with Dr David Cutler, Kew's head of plant anatomy, called *Tree Roots and Buildings*, which drew on the results of a questionnaire sent out to engineers, surveyors, and loss adjusters who were investigating tree root problems.

"We were able to tabulate how far the roots of different sorts of trees had been known to cause damage to buildings, so that gave me

Trees and shrubs in the garden may be desirable but they also need to be kept under control. No one is more aware of their hidden dangers than DR IAN RICHARDSON who has made a career out of studying the roots of trees and shrubs which have caused subsidence damage. Since he started Richardson's Botanical Identifications in Reading 18 years ago, the dry summers have caused a boom in business

the practical experience to start up on my own in 1979," said Ian.

When the insurance companies made the far-reaching decision in 1972 to include subsidence damage in their insurance cover, it led to an ever-growing need to identify the trees which were causing damage to buildings. Really bad subsidence can amount to thousands of pounds worth of damage.

"Apart from creating big cracks, the ultimate horror is that the house might fall down," said Ian. "When the internal as well as external walls of the house are affected, the house has to be underpinned inside and out. All the carpets and floors have to be taken up and the occupiers have to be moved out to a hotel or equivalent accommodation for three to six months. If you've got a big house in Hampstead, your underpinning costs could vary from £10,000 up to £150,000."

With figures like that, correct identification of the tree or shrub responsible is vital and Ian is one of the few experts in the field. His motives in setting up his own business were largely domestic – he wanted to spend more time at home in Reading as his children grew up – and he thought, modestly, "there was the potential to make a bit of money out of it if we did have a few droughts. I knew there would be good years and bad years and so I thought I would make a go of it." He had no idea of quite how many good years there would be.

"This work goes up and down enormously, depending on whether we have had a dry summer or a wet summer," he explained. "That is because clay soils, unlike any other sort of soil, change their volume depending on whether they're wet or dry; drying clay soil shrinks so a house built on clay goes down and may suffer subsidence damage. Lots of houses in London, in other big cities, in fact all over England, are built on clay for various reasons, so if you've got trees within

Diagram of a cross-section of a lime
(Tilia) root by Rowena Gale

rooting range and you have a dry summer, you get a lot of subsidence claims."

Ian's 'work phenomenon', as he calls it, really took off in 1989, with the first of the real drought years, closely followed by 1990/91, 1995 and 1996. These long hot, dry summers, directly related to the greenhouse effect, caused an overwhelming increase in Ian's work load.

What happens in a drought year is that trees lose a lot more water out of their leaves into the air (a phenomenon called evapotranspiration) than in a wet summer. A big tree with a lot of leaves has to get its water from somewhere and so the roots take up water from the soil. The water does not stay in the tree. Within two or three hours, 99.9 per cent of the water has gone through the surface of the leaves and disappeared into the atmosphere. A big tree takes hundreds of gallons of water a day from the soil out into the air. In a dry summer, as the soil dries up the roots have to spread further and deeper for water so they become more of a threat to the houses which come within range of the newly spreading roots.

The Kew tree root survey showed that the worst types of trees for damage were oak, poplar, and willow – elm had been bad before Dutch Elm Disease intervened. "Much more recently trees of increasing importance in the landscape, such as the eucalyptus, native to Australia, are cropping up. Eucalyptus's root activity is quite worrying.

"There are some Mediterranean trees in Britain which you might also expect to be very active in dry summers but they're not necessarily so; horse chestnut for example is a tree from the Balkan Peninsula and yet it's not one of the worst. The safest trees are birches, some of the smaller trees and conifers – unless people put a row of conifers a metre from their wall and then forget to trim them

Elms are no longer the problem they were

and suddenly they're up to the roof and the owners have got a subsidence problem.

"The other main criterion is the size of the tree. An 8m apple tree is probably as bad as an 8m-tall ash but of course the ash is going to grow a lot bigger and therefore a lot more aggressive. If you keep a tree small, then it's not going to be such a threat as if you let it go and become a very big tree."

When Ian started his business he was on his own, with only one other person in the country doing similar work, an Oxford professor. "The two of us used to discuss roots over the phone. When he died in 1989, it coincided with a huge increase in work and for a while I was the only person in the country offering this service. Suddenly I had over 4,000 jobs waiting to be done and a six-month delay but I couldn't turn the work away. As a result, a few others began to offer the service and there are now possibly about ten nationwide although I still do the lion's share of the work."

The horse chestnut is not one of the greediest trees

Until recently Ian was working from home but with the huge increase in work he had to move to a purpose-built laboratory on the University of Reading campus to cope with all the paperwork. Roots – sometimes as many as 100 a day – come from all over the country, wherever there is clay soil, particularly London, Kent, Essex, and up the Thames Valley. Over the past five years there has been a noticeable increase in the amount of work coming from the Midlands and the North. The more recent droughts have hit them as well as the South and there is an an increasing awareness of subsidence problems in the North.

"We try and do a seven-day turnaround but when we are very busy we can't just take on extra staff to cope with it – it's so specialised – so we have to work harder and try and keep up," said Ian.

"I rely heavily on Rowena Gale who works for me three days a week. She is a plant archaeologist who was on the anatomy staff at Kew with me. She is the only other person who can competently identify roots at a decent speed to make it viable.Three people prepare the microscope slides by sectioning the roots but then you reach the bottleneck. These roots are sitting waiting to be examined under the microscope and that's totally up to me and Rowena.

"Ideally roots should be about a pencil thickness but a lot of the people investigating subsidence take boreholes with augers and they get out horrible scrappy bits of root, often a millimetre in diameter, but we manage even though it's much harder and slower identifying really tiny pieces.

"We can identify most trees pretty quickly but we do get bogged down on some of the shrubs; there are so many of them and their root structure isn't as well documented. We can usually narrow them down. We commonly get about 20 main sorts of tree root – because with root identification it's not possible to go down to the species – and then we get things like tulip trees or Indian bean trees which are relatively rare. Shrubs like rose or honeysuckle occur very frequently but there are a lot of shrubs which are much rarer. There must be 50-odd shrubs which we can recognise as well as 30 trees which we receive relatively frequently. There's another 100 or so which we still debate before reaching a decision.

"It always tends to be busiest from October onwards because the 'nasties' have built up in the summer and people come back from their August holiday to find cracks in their house. The claims go through and it's usually October or November when they reach us."

The 'cure' is not always drastic. Nowadays insurance companies or loss adjusters tend to advise that a tree is severely reduced in leaf –

"Shrubs are beginning to be considered of some importance and the National House Building Council is doing some research into their effect. I think shrubs usually work in conjunction with a tree. Again it is the size which is important. Overgrown hedges, crowded bushes or trees are more dangerous than they would be individually."

perhaps by a half or two-thirds – rather than removed. This will curtail its root activity for a few years but will need doing again."

Busy though he is now, Ian believes the work will not go on forever. "There is a limit to vulnerable houses with trees in silly places although I think that hasn't yet been reached. The phenomenon has been known by the public in the south-east of England for 20 years, and building societies' surveyors are now very aware of trees nearby. Over the next 10 years the potential for problems might well go down, but of course we still have the greenhouse effect, and that is an unknown quantity."

Whatever happens, Ian will be calling it a day.

"I nearly stopped this summer; it's crazy but I'll probably stay for another two or three years. I'll just give up with a shriek one day and my son James may take over. When I stop I want to go back to my original research into wild plants of North Africa. An increased knowledge of such areas will assist in conservation projects – and in turn, perhaps in combatting the greenhouse effect which has been so beneficial to me!"

'MUCH REMAINS UNSUNG'

Nor taste alone and well-contriv'd diplay
Suffice to give the marshall'd ranks the grace
Of their complete effect. Much yet remains
Unsung, and many cares are yet behind,
And more laborious; cares on which depend
Their vigour, injur'd soon, not soon restor'd.
The soil must be renew'd, which, often wash'd,
Loses its treasure of salubrious salts,
And disappoints the roots; the slender roots
Close interwoven, where they meet the vase,
Must smooth be shorn away; the sapless branch
Must fly before the knife; the wither'd leaf
Must be detach'd, and where it strews the floor
Swept with a woman's neatness, breeding else
Contagion, and disseminating death.
Discharge but these kind offices, (and who
Would spare, that loves them, offices like these?)
Well they reward the toil. The sight is pleas'd,
The scent regal'd, each odorif'rous leaf,
Each op'ning blossom, freely breathes abroad
Its gratitude, and thanks him with its sweets.

William Cowper
The Task (Book III)
The Garden (603-62)

r for roses

A bed of roses

Someone once said life is like a bowl of cherries – maybe some of the time. A bed of roses is another saying which comes to mind, indeed we have such a bed in our country cottage garden, one which came into being the autumn after our spring wedding in 1990. It stands within a circle of look-alike blocks of Cotswold stone – Cotswold because that's where we spent our older persons' honeymoon.

It was a wet and windy week as I recall, but weather we managed almost to ignore as we visited, investigated and otherwise enjoyed the places of interest the Cotswolds are famed for. The gas fire of 'logs' in the lounge of our small hotel was always a welcome sight in the evening. When we returned to our home we then enjoyed several weeks of superb sunshine, such is the contrary side of our weather systems.

Our particular bed of roses eventually evolved from wedding gifts of garden vouchers and roses with romantic names. It consists of one standard surrounded by free-flowering floribunda all nurtured with compatible compost, libations of liquid and pruned as prescribed. Seven years on the original labels are long gone to ground but the roses survive to bloom with abundance through each summer, an annual delight to the senses of sight and smell.

Mind you, back in 1987 my life had become anything but a bed of roses. After the sudden death of my beloved husband of 30 years, life

When SHEILA PLANK remarried, her late-flowering romance was celebrated by family and friends with wedding gifts of garden vouchers and roses with romantic names. The rose beds continue to bloom in the garden of her Silchester cottage, a reminder of a happy anniversary

felt more like a thicket of thorns. He had worked for a builder and somehow our garden had become a storage area for building materials of all kinds and anything remotely floral was purely accidental. After initial grieving, I felt a stirring of a horticultural nature and over that first summer of widowhood I slowly reclaimed that garden.

Away went the building materials and in came assorted plant life and a wooden summer-house, self-carpentered wooden planters filling odd corners. When I left that garden three years later it had indeed become a pleasant place to be. I had become a born-again gardener and surprisingly enough had felt the stirrings of a romantic nature and married another gardener, a man I would previously have been unable to wed. Why? Because my second spouse, a widower, was my brother-in-law, 'prohibited kin' until an alteration to the Matrimonial Causes Act in 1949 or thereabouts.

Thus it was I was wooed and wed on Easter Saturday 1990, a truly family affair with everyone in full wedding rig, myself in a flowing ivory-coloured gown. The wedding took place in my local church and my son gave me away. My new husband's son was his best man, and my seven grandchildren (four girls and three boys) acted as bridesmaids and escorts.

Drawn by Romilly Swann

As my love and I were in our late fifties a full-dress wedding might have appeared over the top to some. However, we felt such a joyous celebration was an act of faith, showing that people can grieve over the death of a much-loved first partner and, in time, go on to find love and contentment the second time around.

So my spouse and I garden on in contented companionship, and often on a soft summer evening will stop to savour the sight and scent of our very own beautiful bed of roses.

r *for royal berkshire hospital*

Gardens! What gardens?

Most people who come to the Royal Berkshire Hospital are only interested in getting in and out as fast as possible! So they pay little attention to the areas associated with the hospital, things like the gardens – yes, there are gardens.

The gardens are designed for the patients, family and staff to be able to sit in, talk and relax. Within the grounds we have a pond which is very popular with patients in South Wing. It is an area where they can escape from the ward, and any patients who can get down to it will do so.

The area was originally created when South Wing was built in the 1970s, but over the years there have been a few changes which led to the area being left empty and bare. Four years ago we were able to re-fill the pond and stock it with fish. Plants were donated and it became a much more pleasant area for people to enjoy. In fact it is so popular that in rain, shine and even freezing temperatures, you will always find someone out there!

This is only one of a few areas on the hospital site where the patient can get out for just a few minutes, and we hope this helps them on the road to recovery. We are always looking for areas to improve for just this reason. It's a never-ending job gardening...

For me, gardening has been a job since leaving school, starting at Battle Hospital as a gardener, then moving on to the Royal Berkshire about six months later, and now 15 years later I am head gardener.

Even the smallest patch of green has significance. The garden areas of the Royal Berkshire Hospital in Rading mean a great deal to many patients as the head gardener DEREK PROUT tells John Evans, who used to work in the gardens himself and is now an out-patient at the hospital

S *for sutton & sons*

'First house in the trade'

In 1837, Martin Hope Sutton and his brother Alfred established a seed merchants business in the Market Place, Reading. Originally a corn merchants, started by their father, John Sutton, 31 years before, the business became world famous for its unadulterated seed, which it sent carriage free by railway or by penny post all over the UK. With a combination of high standards, shrewd business sense, a readiness to travel worldwide to buy and sell their products, and skilful advertising, Sutton and Sons maintained its position as 'first house in the trade' until the present day.

"At that time there were several things happening which made it a boom time for horticulture," said John Cox, formerly Sutton's company secretary. " One of the things that helped to transform the business was the introduction of the Penny Post in 1840, which meant Sutton's could send small packets of seed by post rather than by carrier."

At the same time, foreign explorers were bringing back new varieties of plants, particularly shrubs and bulbs, which opened up the trade, and in Britain the big landowners were only too eager to stock their estates with exotic new plants.

"Victorians were becoming more prosperous, and the large estates were having more and more money spent on them," explained John. "Everyone wanted to show that they had a grander estate than the next man, so they had bigger gardens and more

For many people, the first sight of Reading was a blaze of colour from the trial grounds of Sutton and Sons, the famous seed merchants which was founded in 1806. It was a sad day for the town when the company moved away to Torquay in 1976. Former employees JOHN COX and GERRY WESTALL, who between them gave nearly 80 years service to Sutton and Sons, talk about the company which, for almost two centuries, has represented the height of horticultural excellence

gardeners. Greenhouses were being introduced and the standards of training and quality of the gardeners were very high."

Up until then the seed trade had been in a bad way. Gerry Westall, another former employee, said: "It was the general practice of people who dealt with seeds in those days to adulterate the seed by mixing dead seed in with it so they could sell more. Of course germination was very poor, whereas now you can say germination is up to 98 per cent depending on the subject. The Sutton family were very upright, religious people, and they were one of the first firms to start testing seeds and really studying germination."

As a result of Sutton's determination to sell pure seed, the Government introduced a Seeds Act, which ensured all seeds were tested and conformed to a certain standard of purity and of germination.

Their seeds travelled all over the world. Gerry said: "The seeds went by ship through the tropics, and as humidity would affect germination they were put in metal tins which were soldered up with a sheet of tin and the lid closed to make the seal airtight. Large consignments were packed into big galvanized metal tanks, which were sealed and could be re-used as water storage tanks.

"This led many years later to Sutton's becoming the first company to put their seeds in foil packets. They were the only company to be given a licence by the Ministry of Agriculture to keep their seeds in the packets for three years, although they would still test them each year."

Sutton's was a forward-looking business which recognised the power of advertising. John recalled: "On every railway station there was a large enamelled sign saying 'Sutton Seeds from Reading, no agents,' with the slogan 'best in the world'. The railway bridge by Sutton Industrial Estate had one of these signs for many years."

The publicity paid off. In 1858 Queen Victoria ordered Martin Hope to supply seeds to the royal household. "This was before the

The seed trade was a gentlemanly business in the old days. Sutton's representatives would visit the great estates in November to get the next year's order from the head gardener. The rep would give the gardener his new diary and ask for a cheque for last year's account and the gardener would then have a year's credit. There was always a great demand for gardeners on these big estates and often employers would write to Sutton and Sons and ask them to recommend a suitable foreman or a head gardener. Of course Sutton's could recommend a man who bought Sutton's seeds and that would be another part of his loyalty. If the job turned out well, when the Sutton's representative called next season the gardener would be reminded how he got the job so he wouldn't buy seeds from a rival firm.

present system of royal warrant was instituted," explained John. "After that the firm applied for and was awarded the royal warrant. Martin Hope made several visits to the royal gardens at Windsor and to Osborne, on the Isle of Wight, where Queen Victoria's children had their own gardens. He would advise them, doffing his top hat, an impressive sight. Again it was very good publicity – very shrewd."

Sutton's used personal recommendation very extensively in advertising to stay ahead of its competitors. Who could fail to be impressed when the gardener to the Duke of Bedfordshire informed Mr Sutton that he had "a full basket of peas last year and had a wonderful crop, highly recommended to all Mr Sutton's customers", or when the Chamberlain to His Majesty the King of Denmark, wrote: "100 acres of grass seeds sent to me last autumn were good. They were sowed in spring and came up well." Other recommendations came from as far afield as New Zealand and India. One customer from abroad sent a rather backhanded compliment: "The seeds were very good, in fact they germinated so freely that half the contents I ordered would have been sufficient."

Sutton's started travelling abroad in the mid-1880s to buy new and better quality strains, and new varieties. The Suttons and their most experienced staff would inspect the crops to make sure there was no cross-pollination and the plants were true to type. The grower would then send the seed to Reading and Sutton's would clean and test the seeds on their trial grounds at Earley. As the business prospered and expanded, more trial grounds were acquired in Slough in

In the Spring catalogue of 1875, Sutton's declared: "We believe we were the first house in the trade, and for many years the only one, which directly opposed the practice of mixing dead seed with good and there can be no doubt that our supplying the public with genuine seeds, which in results gave so great a contrast to adulterated seeds, was the means of stopping, to a certain extent, the discreditable practice so long maintained. We take the opportunity to repeat what we said 12 years ago that never during the many years that we have been in business have we ever mixed dead seeds with good and that we never intend to do so, whatever competition in prices may occur."

Sutton & Sons' business premises as they used to be in the centre of Reading

1913 and Cornwall after World War Two. Other land was rented at the historic Southcote Manor, which had cabbages nestling incongruously on the edge of the moat.

For many years Sutton's main shop and all the administration and business offices and warehouses covered a huge area at the Market Place site, part of which was once the garden of the old Reading Abbey. A large portion belonged to the Blagrave family.

"Sutton's had six or seven acres behind the shop, a veritable warren of passages and corridors" said Gerry. "It was a most uneconomical building to maintain and keep warm in the winter, as we knew to our cost, though probably no worse than a lot of others."

"But it was a wonderful place for boys," said John, "because they could lose themselves in there all day and you could never find them in all those passageways. If a fire had started, the centre of Reading would have gone up in flames."

The end of the splendid Sutton's site was 'a tragedy', said John. "The Minister of Transport decided to put an inner ring road, through part of The Forbury, which would have gone right through the back of Sutton's warehouse, and across Kings Road. They had to get out quickly so they exchanged their freehold site for a new building at their trial grounds, in Earley, in 1962. But the sad thing, of course, was the Inner Ring Road never materialised so Sutton's could have stayed there anyway."

As it turned out, the new location had many advantages, and probably most people who live in Reading or who ever travelled to Reading will remember Sutton's at the trial grounds.

John said: "There were about 60 acres, bought in the 1870s partly

Cabbages growing round Southcote Manor, which was demolished in 1921

Sutton's had a horse-drawn fire engine in the 1880s and ran their own fire brigade with company employees. This was essential bearing in mind the amount of timber used in their premises. During the Second World War, they had a Coventry Climax trailer pump, which was kept near the cycle sheds at the Abbey Square entrance.

from George Palmer and partly from Viscount Sidmouth, who lived at Sidmouth Grange, just across the main London Road. Sutton's used it as a trial ground because it was a wonderful situation, on the outskirts of Reading so that their staff could live in the Victorian terrace houses of Newtown.

"It had another great advantage.When people were travelling on either the old Great Western line from Reading to Paddington, or on the Southern line to Waterloo and Guildford, they could see the trial grounds and the acres of sweet peas and other flowers. It was a wonderful advertisement."

Another landmark were the superb greenhouses, built towards the end of the last century, and in their day the height of modern construction with the main pavilion made of teak and cast iron. Sadly these historic buildings had to make way for Suttons industrial estate.

"When Sutton's moved from Reading to Torquay in 1976, some of us stayed behind to set up another company in Charvil selling seeds to market growers," said Gerry. "We hadn't been up there many days when a man from London rang and said, 'I've got a client who's interested in buying your old greenhouse pavilion facing the railway on the old trial grounds site.' He was just too late – it had been bulldozed a couple of days before, the whole lot, and all the cast iron had been removed."

John had started work for Sutton and Sons in 1932 at the age of 16, and remained there for 44 years working his way up to become company secretary. "Jobs were very very scarce, and it just happened that Sutton's had a job, at 16 shillings a week.

Sutton's had a very active recreation club for women and men, with a sports ground in Cintra Avenue, off Christchurch Road. Employees played cricket, football, bowls, hockey, lacrosse, tennis and archery, and there was an angling section which was started in 1879. At the main building in Market Place there was a superb billiard table, and at the trial grounds a bowling green grown, of course, from Sutton's seeds.

Sutton's vegetable seed order room

I lived at Newbury and I had to pay for the train fare. I was an office boy in the invoice office, running with pieces of paper. As long as you had a piece of paper in your hand and you could say where you were going, you were safe.

"I remember there was a commissionaire on the door in the Market Place, an Irish ex-guardsman, with a waxed moustache, who wore a blue uniform, with initials on his round hat, SS – Sutton and Sons. His duty was to open and close the door at the main front entrance. He was very formidable and dealt with any boys playing around the entrance. You weren't allowed to go through that entrance unless you were on the salaried staff. You had to go round the back into the Forbury entrance or the Abbey Square."

There was an all-male staff until the 1930s (except for the pea-pickers who were usually widows). Gerry started in the dispatch office in 1944, at the age of 14, and remained there working in various departments finishing as trade office manager. He recalled: "When I first went there, they had an air-raid shelter at the back of the potato department by the Holy Brook, so if the building had been hit you would never have got out; you would either have been drowned or you would have been suffocated! We also had strengthened cellars but we were never anywhere near them so it would have been hard to shelter there if there had been a raid."

This potato department was joined to the main building by a bridge across Abbey Square. It was here the seed potatoes were selected, graded for size and stored. They were grown in Scotland, sent down to Reading by lorry and train and stored there safely away from frost before being dispatched .

When John and Gerry were working there, Sutton's were employing 200 to 250 full-timers, and many more 'permanent temporaries', part-time staff who packaged seeds in the autumn and dispatched them in the spring.

The Sutton family were enlightened employers who took their

In 1847 the Irish potato crop failed due to potato blight fungus. The British Government ordered large quantities of turnip, cabbage and other seeds. In response, Sutton's sent large consignments of quick maturing vegetable seed.

employees' welfare to heart. John said: "Prayers were taken, usually by the vicar of St Laurence, in a room at the firm. It was voluntary but the family were very religious and they thought that was right for their employees. On occasions when there wasn't a vicar, Martin Sutton used to take this service because he was a lay preacher."

The firm started a pension fund in 1920 and they had a burial fund, and a sick fund into which employees paid sixpence a week. Years ahead of their time, they banned smoking in the workplace on health grounds and as a fire hazard, and provided paid holidays.

Gerry said: "When they had a day's outing, to places like the Isle of Wight, Sutton's booked a whole train for the staff and their wives. On the way back, the Directors used to walk up and down the platform looking in the carriages to see if any of them had had too much to drink. The old boys inside would be trying to sit up straight and look sober."

Although Sutton's continued to prosper up until the Second World War, changes in society took their toll on the seed trade. The great estates had gone, and with them the gardeners. People had smaller gardens, and less time and money to spend on them. In recent years the trend moved sharply away from seeds towards bedding plants and the seed companies which are now left all sell vegetable and flower plants.

Unfortunately there are no Suttons at Sutton's any more. The business was taken over by Mr Douglas Collins, who had previously founded the famous Goya perfume company. It is now part of a conglomerate of European companies.

At its peak, Sutton's was a household name, a large local employer which not only tested and sold seeds, flowers and bulbs but built and designed gardens and golf courses. It was a world in itself, and a world that has now passed away.

The Sutton family had more tragedy to bear than many during the Great War. Leonard Sutton had become chairman of the company and lost four of his five sons in the Great War. The effect was devastating to the family and the business, the more so as two of these sons had undertaken extensive business travels to Australia and New Zealand and had started a new venture by establishing a subsidiary company in Calcutta, India.

Prizewinners – thanks to Sutton's seeds, in the Royal East Berks Agricultural Association 1925

Trial grounds remembered

Quaint to think about it, but already we have a generation of Reading people who have no memory of the days of Sutton's Seed Trial Grounds in London Road, Earley, a site which is now just another light industrial estate.

One could argue that the departure of that company to Torquay brought about the most malignant scenic disaster that the town of Reading has had to undergo. Indeed, it cannot be wrong to say that, with the demise of those grounds, an entire dimension of the borough was lost too. No building on earth could match that vision of beauty, as everyone who ever passed through Reading by rail during the summertime until 1976 will have seen for themselves.

My own experience of those colour-filled acres started in 1965 when I began working on the trial grounds as a horticultural assistant, and by the time of the company closure I had become the grounds' foreman. Here, chosen as much for their variety as for their vividness, are just a few of my memories.

The boundless beauty of certain of the flower-seed crops that were tended throughout the year. Different colours, different stature, different shapes, different habits too. Was there anything I did not love? I cannot think of a single example. My own top favourite – even above the pink scabious that attracted so many butterflies in August – was the September-flowering rock purslane (*Calandrinia umbellata*) which, from its compact, dark-green leaf cushions, gave such a spectacular

BERNARD REDWAY was foreman of Sutton and Sons' trial grounds at the time that they closed in 1976. He has vivid memories of those days

The large centrepiece conservatory faced the Grat Western Railway. From both sides a range of glass ran parallel to the railway, from which at right angles radiated a further range of glasshouses

Plants and flowers (above Vanda sp) of the tropical rainforest at Hampstead Norreys painted by Romilly Swann. Story on page 125.

Above: Horticultural Therapy's Trunkwell Park project. Story on page 158.

The Plough on the Green pub at Newbury has a prizewinning garden. Story on page 118.

Numberplate 9 created by Michael from the Offshoots project, at Englefield. Story on page 106.

display with its massed, cupped blooms of shouting magenta – but only when the sun shone.

Rapping out the various seeds onto the heavy, brown dust sheets that were spread on the barn floor, using a stick that had been cut from the ash trees that grew nearby. An apparently out-dated method, but it made for a high yield and gave the staff something to do during the winter months or whenever it was raining.

Getting behind the great rear wheels of vehicles – usually tractors but on one occasion a slab transporter, and for this task I was acting alone – in order to push them free from the dark jaws of the mud that came with every wet spell.

Celery beds at the trial grounds

Noting 26 species of butterflies and far more moths, using my lunch hour to extend my exploration of the grounds and the adjacent Western Region railway embankment.

Standing on the topmost rung of a ladder when that rung suddenly snapped clean at both ends. I just managed to jam my fingers into the bark of the elm tree I had been lopping, so preventing a headlong backward fall to the ground beneath. Very soon afterwards I hurled this over-aged and life-threatening contrivance onto a large bonfire.

Coping with the noise level when attempting to hold a conversation. Bounded by two railways, a busy main road and an arterial flight path, the trial grounds at times gave the impression of having been carefully placed for maximum sound interference.

Having to use, during a spell of extreme staff shortage, two hoes at once in order to shape up a great bed of seedlings. The tool used was the short-handled onion hoe and one was held in each hand.

One of my particular responsibilities was to cut the grounds' hedges. The implement I had to use, powered by a compressor attached to a tractor, was highly temperamental, and one of its many drawbacks was that its barrel would freeze up inside and bring progress to a halt even when the air temperature was some degrees above freezing-point. To combat this problem I would tie a sack around the tractor's exhaust chimney, then, once warmed up, I would tie that sack around the cutter's barrel. Another sack would next be tied around the chimney to take over from the first sack once it had cooled, and so on. How many passers-by, I thought, misread the situation and wondered why I was lagging the chimney itself, and at a time when the tractor's engine was running at full throttle!

At times there were mercy missions. I remember having to evacuate thousands of caterpillars (such as Small Tortoiseshells and Peacocks) from nettle clumps that I had been instructed to spray with weedkiller, and on another occasion I warned someone I saw gathering groundsel to feed her budgerigars or canaries, that I had sprayed those plants earlier in the day; this would have proved fatal to her entire aviary of seventy birds, she said.

After Sutton's moved to Torquay I continued working on the site as a landscape gardener for a further four years and I was given the task of demolishing certain of the wooden buildings and sheds. One such structure, about the size of an average house, I felled with a sledgehammer, knocking in all the supporting uprights at their bases except just one on each long side and at the middle of the building, then putting my back against the centre of its south side and shoving to the limit of my strength. Moments later, what had been towering above me stood at nothing more than about knee level. As the dust clouds settled in the calm bright air above the site that had once been the Laboratory Garden, I was aware of having just taken part in an event that marked the end of an era for both of us.

SOUND ADVICE

Cut the necks and shoulders from plastic lemonade bottles and use the remainder as cloches for single plants.

Canes that are less than head-high are a constant danger to the gardener. A small upturned plastic flower pot or a bored cork placed on top of the cane may prevent a serious eye injury.

Regular dead-heading will invariably prolong the flowering period as plants will continue to bloom in their efforts to produce seed.

Shady areas of the garden need not be abandoned in despair to ivy and fern. Many attractive and unusual plants including hellebores, astrantias some varieties of the hardy geranium – as well as the even less common blue poppy (*Meconopsis grandis*), trillium and Turk's-cap lily (*Lilium martagon*) will exist quite happily under tree cover.

Before setting light to bonfires, check thoroughly for hibernating hedgehogs and other wildlife.

S *for sutton's bowling club*

A bias towards flowers

It's the last match of the outdoor bowling season. In Lower Earley, the heart of the biggest private housing estate in Europe, is an unexpected patch of colour, the almost unreal brightness of the perfectly kept bowling-green surrounded by thirteen brick-built flowerbeds, each filled with flowers.

These beds, built by bricklayer Reg Norriss, are much in demand. Members queue up for the privilege of looking after one. They surround three sides of the green, on two sides against the fence and on the side facing the clubhouse, with open fencing behind so local people using the public footpath can see what's going on. Reg built wooden backings to the beds to show the flowers to better advantage and some have been used to display hanging baskets.

The flowerbeds are all individual, reflecting the tastes of their gardeners, some carefully co-ordinated, others more flamboyant. One bed mixes sweet peas, dahlias, sunflowers – and a model ape.

The flowerbeds are an innovation introduced when the club moved in 1989. Sutton's original bowling-green was at the Sutton's Seeds site, near the centre of Reading, where it was a show-piece, looking like a green carpet, and helping to sell Sutton's grass seed. When the site was due to be redeveloped, Wokingham District Council relocated the club to Lower Earley, built the shell of the clubhouse and laid the green. Since then Sutton's members have done everything including building the bar and furnishing it.

SUTTON'S BOWLING CLUB was started in 1906 for employees of Sutton's Seeds in Reading, and although it no longer has any links with the company since it moved to Torquay, Sutton's retained the name and is a successful and flourishing club with more than 200 playing members, about 70 social members – and a waiting list. It blooms in other ways too, as MARGARET KELLY explains, and visiting bowlers are astonished by the colourful display which greets them when they step onto the green

Peter Swinn, a member of the club since 1986, said: "The gardens were a committee idea to brighten the place up a bit. We are in the middle of this huge housing estate and when you walk through the front door it is quite impressive to see the flowers. It is traditional in bowling clubs to have floral displays, but nothing like these. I don't think there is another bowling club in Berkshire like it."

The flowerbed gardeners pay for their own plants and for looking after their own gardens. Women, who at one time were not allowed on the green, predominate among the gardeners. "We are still segregated," laughed Betty Reed, a member of the women's section which was started in 1979. "Men come first in the bowling world but the ladies come first in the gardening.

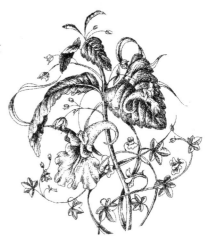

"It's a talking point. Everybody who comes to play says how nice the gardens look. People from other clubs come along and take the seed pods. Lady bowlers have been known to say 'I like those sweet peas, I'll take some of those'. When you are standing on the edge of the green they will say, 'I've got a pocket full of seeds!' If they picked them just as we were going to bowl, I think we'd kick their ankles!"

Pam Woodcock and Pat Cooper have shared a flowerbed for about six years. Pat said: "The idea for the gardens came when the club was being built here and they wanted something that was easily kept. There was no natural space for flowerbeds so Reg Norriss built the beds of brick and we filled them up with soil and fertiliser. We fought over the beds. Even now if one looks tatty, we ask, 'Are you going to keep that bed?'"

"It's easier to share," said Pam. "We consult each other about what we're going to put in."

They agreed that in the first year their bed was very 'higgledy piggledy', they put in whatever was in the greenhouse – tall daisies, marigolds, pansies – which was a disaster.

Pam said: "I tend to look for a packet of seeds which is a bit different from the norm. We've got Marvel of Peru, the Four o'clock plant, with a little tiny flower. It's fragrant early in the morning and goes off later in the day. It should be called Morning Glory."

The beds tend to dry out so they decided geraniums and begonia would do better than lobelia. Pat said: "It's tricky to keep it watered, but when you're away people will do it for you. We're competitive people but in a friendly way and nobody would see somebody else's flowers die"

Betty Reed took over a bed in 1996. "I liked everybody else's garden and I thought I would do something different but it didn't work my first year. I thought I would have an ornament in the middle, a bowl on a stand, so that all the flowers would trail down the side but the centrepiece was drunk and would not stand up properly. I tried a red, white and blue colour scheme, sort of patriotic, but when the flowers came through, I got pink, brown and yellow! I'm not a very good gardener but I thoroughly enjoy doing it."

Sheila Tibbles, a bowling member for five years, shares a corner plot with her husband, Roy. It was one of the last beds to be built: "Usually you have to wait till somebody gives up, but we were lucky enough to get one of the two new ones. It was great fun planning it. We have put in three dwarf conifers, wallflowers in assorted colours, grown from seed, and groups of daffodils – we don't lift them. We put them in about 12 inches deep and there is a chance they'll flower here or in Australia."

As they are semi-retired, Sheila and Roy can come during the week to care for their bed, and often visit five times a week. "Obviously as you walk round during a bowls match or if you've finished bowling, you'll notice a couple of weeds which need to come out. It depends which way you're bowling. You don't do the garden when you're bowling! It doesn't look right!"

This is a specialised form of gardening and all the bowlers have learned by their mistakes. Pat Cooper said she was determined to start with bigger plants so they had colour in the beds quickly. Frost

"We did hope we would be able to expand and have another bowling green but the council have built a large clubhouse there for football and cricket so there is no room for expansion. But we are a go-ahead club and we are always looking to improve our facilities for members. The main thing we spend our money on is the bowling-green, it costs thousands of pounds a year for maintaining that. And it's paid for by all us drinkers indirectly. It's all voluntary, nobody gets paid. Our income comes from the bar."
Peter Swinn

is the danger in early May, when the season starts, although the beds are fairly well sheltered.

Pat said: "As you can see, we enjoy our flowerbeds and we have some fun. One guy kept getting black spot on his roses. Somebody told him to dig banana skins underneath, which are actually very good for roses; the other tip was to get a garlic and plant it upside down in his garden which he duly did. He wasn't a particularly good gardener so we took the mickey and said he'd got garlic-scented roses!

"People from other clubs always remark on our lovely gardens and I've never come across a bowling club like ours."

A VISIT TO SWALLOWFIELD

John Evelyn wrote in his diary on October 22, 1685, about a visit to Swallowfield Park which had been rebuilt in 1678 for Henry Hyde, Viscount Cornbury, later 2nd Earl of Clarendon. He acquired the estate through his marriage in 1670 to Flower, daughter and heiress of Mr William Backhouse, of Swallowfield.

'I accompanied my Lady Clarendon to her house in Swallowfield, in Berkshire... this house is after the ancient building of honourable gentlemen's houses, when they kept up ancient hospitality, but the gardens and waters, as elegant as it is possible to make a flat by art and industry, and no mean expense, my lady being so extraordinarily skilled in the flowery part, and my lord, in diligence of planting; so that I have hardly seen a seat which shows more tokens of it than what is to be found here, not only in the delicious and rarest fruits of a garden, but in those innumerable timber trees in the ground about the seat, to the greatest ornament and benefit of the place.

There is one orchard of 1000 golden, and other cider pippins; walks and groves of elms, limes, oaks, and other trees.

The garden is so beset with all manner of sweet shrubs, that it perfumes the air. The distribution also of the quarters, walks, and parterres, is excellent. The nurseries, kitchen-garden full of the most desirable plants; two very noble orangeries well furnished; but, above all, the canal and fish ponds...The waters are flagged about with *Calamus aromaticus*, with which my lady has hung a closet, that retains the smell very perfectly.

There is also a certain sweet willow and other exotics; also a very fine bowling green, meadow, pasture, and wood: in a word, all that can render a country seat delightful.'

t *for st teresa's school*

The chequerboard garden

Nicola Wright: In February 1996, our chequerboard garden was not a chequerboard garden. It was only a patch of grass in our field. How were we to know that soon that small square of grass between Miss Brown's classroom and the kitchen was to become a beautiful garden?

Anushka Fernando: It all started in February 1996, when there was a staff meeting. All the teachers came with their big books to the meeting. Then Mrs Power (our headteacher) started to discuss with the teachers about a square garden. Mrs Hall (one of the teachers) came up with a brilliant idea: she thought of a chequerboard square garden. All the teachers and Mrs Power were satisfied and thought that was a great idea. It took them a long time to find the right place for the garden. It had to have sun and a place where there was not much wind. Finally we found a place near the kitchen and one classroom where some grass was. The reason why they did this garden was for the children to enjoy it.

Robert Cooper: The chequerboard was going to be square-shaped paving slab, space for plant, paving slab, space for plant and so on. There were seven rows (a row for each class) and each row was going to have three or four squares.

There was a letter sent out asking for dads to help make the chequerboard garden. My dad applied to help. So there it was, all planned out. The Bycroft family gave the school 25 paving slabs for

The beautiful chequerboard garden in the school grounds is a source of delight to children at St TERESA'S RC PRIMARY SCHOOL, in Wokingham, but the project needed careful planning and a lot of hard work as three of the pupils explain

the chequerboard garden. The Lloyd family very kindly gave the sundial to the school. The school bought some edging for the garden.

Nicola: April 1996 and the hot sun shone down on our school. It was a Saturday morning and the workers were already hard at work. The teachers had been thinking about the garden since February and had decided that this would be a good day to do it. So that day Mrs Hall (my teacher), Mrs Power (headteacher) and four or five dads gave up their lazy Saturday morning to make our chequerboard garden.

Robert: They had to use a spring-back tape-measure to measure where exactly they wanted the chequerboard garden. They had to be careful, making sure they measured properly or everything would go wrong.

Nicola: First they had to clear away the grass (which was then laid on the field's 'bald spot'). The earth then had to be dug away until the trench was 10 cm deep. You may not think this very deep, but would you like to try digging in VERY hot weather? No, thought not.

The chequerboard garden completed

Cement then had to be mixed, not with a cement mixer but by hand! The cement was put down, then the paving slabs. This was very fiddly work because each paving slab had to be absolutely flat, and the length of one slab had to be measured between each slab.

Anushka: Then they worked on one of the squares from the corner and started measuring a gap. After they had done the first row it was easier because the first row had four slabs, so the next one would have three slabs and four spaces. They worked their way through and finally finished.

Nicola: A border of long, grey bricks was laid round the length of the garden to give it a finishing touch. But no, it still wasn't finished.

One sunny day, at 12 pm, Mr Dearden (school caretaker) and Mrs Hall placed a sundial on the middle slab. Mr Dearden twisted it round until the shadow was in line with the point. It was then cemented down.

Each class was then given one row to grow things in. This is what each class grew in their row:

Class 1B, 1G, Flowers for cutting

Class 2, Bulbs

Class 3, Herbs

Class 4, Vegetables

Class 5, Alpine plants

Class 6, Bedding plants

The garden has been very popular since it was built and every so often each class goes and tends their row.

Anushka: After some time we entered the garden for the Mayor's garden competition. A few days passed and Mrs Power and other children went up to the Town Hall and we were presented with a certificate. We came second and were highly commended. We also were in the newspapers for our garden.

Nicola: We are very proud of this garden since it is mostly our work. It also has a lot of different things in it, as you have seen from the list. It seems always at its best at summer, since most of the plants are flowers.

Last year, in Class 4, we grew some massive beans and quite big potatoes. They were then sold at the festival sale.

I hope you enjoyed reading about our chequerboard garden, and I'd just like to say the garden was a lot of fun and we all think the hard work was worth it!

TIPS FOR A YOUNG GARDENER

Listen to everything that older gardeners tell you because there is no substitute for experience; but never be afraid to experiment; that's the way the older gardeners gained their experience. Try everything; and if someone tells you that that particular task is impossible, try a little harder.

Professor Stefan Buczacki

t *for thatcham*

Auntie May's Garden

My Auntie May was a maiden lady who lived with her father – my grandfather – who was a watchmaker, jeweller and engraver in Thatcham. He worked up to his eighties, and then he moved into this big house, I think it was called Broadway House, at 50 The Broadway. It had a cellar, which was a most intriguing place, and this lovely garden.

Auntie May wasn't very old when her mother died, and she helped Grandpa to bring up the rest of the family, my mother included – ten children altogether. She had an eventful life. She was most interested in the total abstinence movement, and she went off to America and travelled all over the country preaching about the evils of drink. She knew the President's wife, Mrs Eleanor Roosevelt, who was also a great prohibitionist, and kept in touch with her.

My grandpa and aunt were staunch supporters of the Congregational Church. Auntie May did the flowers every week for the church, and I used to go and help her, doing the menial things, like polishing the large copper jug that she used. She always seemed to be able to produce flowers, lovely Madonna lilies, delphiniums, daisies. When the family had grown up, she divided her time between helping Grandpa in the shop, and working in this garden which took up quite a lot of time. She spent many hours there.

It was such a haven in those days; when I think of Thatcham Broadway as it is now… You went through the house, out into the

GLADYS BRADFORD

GLADYS BRADFORD, has happy memories of a garden in Thatcham, which was a haven for her as a young girl from Australia

courtyard, and then through the gate into the long, rambling garden. It was quite magical really. It was like heaven to me. Coming from Australia, I'd never seen such lovely plants. She taught me how to discriminate between weeds and her precious plants and to start with I was only trusted to take the daisies out of the lawn. She had a wonderful herbaceous border against the wall, facing south – it must have been 60 feet long.

In between was a crazy-paved path and there's a story attached to that. My aunt had what she called a paying guest, a Mr Ted Gall, who worked in the office at the paper mills. Now she really wanted a crazy-paved path to set the garden off, so every evening, after his meal, Mr Gall did about two or three divisions of this path. He carefully put down the little slats of wood, and filled it up with the cement. He had quite a job working out how to fit in all these shapes, I believe. Anyhow he finished it, and it must have been at least 20 yards long. It certainly made a difference to the garden.

Behind the flowers was a kitchen garden. A little old man, a Mr Owen, who rode a tricycle with a spade strapped to the crossbar, used to come and dig it for her.

In those days, there were old-fashioned apples, like Beauty of Bath, lovely red apples, but I wasn't so keen on the taste of them, they were rather sour. There was also a wonderful walnut tree, red-currants, white-currants, and all these things I hadn't seen before.

The Broadway, Thatcham, at the turn of the century. Broadway House, where Mr Charles Brown and his daughter May lived, is on the extreme right

There was a bird bath which was always kept filled so the birds had water, and we had to make sure the cat didn't chase the birds – Spider, the black cat was called. In those days there seemed to be so many more bees and insects humming, and on a hot summer afternoon it was a lovely peaceful place. And to think that this wonderful garden has disappeared under the tarmac of the car-park, and the new shops. It's all gone – even the walnut tree. Not many people would remember it now I suppose.

t *for tittenhurst*

Remembered trees of Tittenhurst

Four hours of enforced idleness when a contractor's machinery broke down enabled Jack Vernon, under the eye of a friendly keeper, to explore the grounds of Tittenhurst Park, a fine old 85-acre estate on the Berkshire-Surrey Border.

It was early in the 1960s and the estate had recently been acquired by Mr Peter Cadbury. Jack Vernon had been working in Silwood Road, close by, and he was particularly interested in the trees on the estate. From the keeper he learned that some of these dated from the time when Thomas Holloway, the manufacturer of patent medicine and founder of Royal Holloway College, had owned the estate and had brought there some unusual and exotic trees.

In particular, he remembers a fine avenue of weeping cherries and an enclosed area devoted to magnolias and some striking camellias. Twelve sequoias were a remarkable sight, quite unlike all previous sequoias he had seen, for these had assumed irregular and curious shapes.

Also in the grounds was a contorted pagoda tree (*Sophora japonica tortuosa*) and, towards the old cricket ground, they found a planting of the golden Indian bean trees (*Catalpas*) and a tall tree which he was unable to identify at the time but which he later learned was a Swedish birch (*Betula pendula* 'Dalecarlica'). Also in the vicinity of the cricket ground was a black oak (*Quercus velutina*) and a tulip tree (*Liriodendron tulipifera*).

Tittenhurst Park, in Sunningdale, is as famous for its trees as its owners who included a millionaire philanthropist and two legendary pop stars. TONY BARHAM relates the story of a local man who gained a rare glimpse of the estate

Several years went by and then, as the park was opened to the public one Sunday afternoon to raise money for the Royal National Lifeboat Institution, Jack Vernon, accompanied by his wife Jean, paid a second visit.

They were particularly interested in two weeping blue cedars (*Cedrus atlantica*) and an unusually tall and shapely incense cedar (*Libocedrus decurrens*), beside a pleasant garden path. They also noticed a statue depicting Artemis with a deer facing towards the house.

Tittenhurst later became the home of John Lennon and it was there that he recorded his famous song 'Imagine', and a video for the song was made in the house and grounds. He sold the house in 1973 and for some years it was the home of Ringo Starr. The shooting and death of Lennon in New York in December 1980 came as a great shock to those who had worked for him at Tittenhurst.

In later years substantial sums have been spent on the house and grounds and security problems made it necessary to restrict access to part of the estate. In spite of the changes it seems that steps have been taken to preserve the more interesting trees and there is now good reason to hope that the Tittenhurst trees will survive to the end of this century and beyond

FOOTNOTE: There is a detailed and accurate article about the Tittenhurst estate by Denis Hardwicke in The Field *(March 26, 1964), with some good black and white photographs. There is more information in the* Gardeners' Chronicle *for 1904.*

A TALE OF TOMATOES

When I was the area surveyor travelling around the then Southern Electricity Board area, I often had to check and survey for new overhead HT lines at and for sewage works and pumping stations. At that time farmers could obtain supplies of dried human manure, as they called it, just like blocks of peat. It was free and odourless. and it was spread over their land. I remember being at one of these sites with another surveyor, a stocky little Londoner and ex-Arnheim veteran, who said, "What are all those plants, matey?"
I replied "Tomato plants." And they were, the most abundant, strong plants. We took some home and eventually picked some really luscious fruit of mixed varieties. It later dawned on us where the seeds came from!
The tomato seed has a good constitution, and whatever happens to it, it can produce some excellent plants!
Gerald Bradford

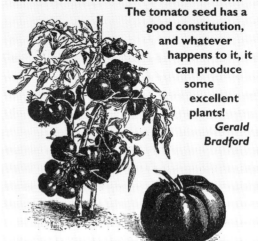

t for trunkwell park

Democracy in the garden

Gardening is therapeutic. It's no secret. At the most basic level, people find it therapeutic go out into their gardens and unwind from the day's work. For many years large institutions and hospitals had their own horticultural departments for patients but most have closed down because of the cost. Now charities like Horticultural Therapy (HT) carry on the work of utilising and promoting this long-recognised benefit of gardening as a form of therapy for people with all kinds of need.

HT was founded in 1978 by a young horticulturist Chris Underhill, inspired by his work with people with learning difficulties and his voluntary service in Africa. He was supported by the Revd Dr Udall, a leading paediatrician at Bart's Hospital, who in 1989 bequeathed his family home, Trunkwell Park, at Beech Hill near Reading, to HT as a teaching and therapeutic centre for people with special needs.

Volunteers from the Friends of Trunkwell, the local support group, cleared the land and started developing two acres of the 180-acre estate to become a centre for horticultural therapy. What was formerly the estate gardens, set around an old courted stable-block, cottage and outbuildings, has now been restored to house a range of facilities including a variety of garden areas, offices, classroom, kitchen and store.

New areas have been cleared and developed by volunteers and

Any time you visit Trunkwell Park, near Reading, you will find people working, busily getting on with jobs on their own or in small groups in the immaculate gardens. The charity Horticultural Therapy which runs the project there, plans eventually to make Trunkwell Park its headquarters

clients working happily together and in the past couple of years the place has been transformed. There is now a Udall Memorial Garden, a nature trail, a wildflower meadow full of poppies, love-in-a-mist and daisies, a sensory garden, a butterfly bed, a pond, a fruit garden, polytunnels, and in the main walled area is a vegetable garden with raised beds and square individual plots all bursting with produce.

"A lot of things we do here are things you could take home with you, that's very important," explained Chris Martin, the project leader and garden manager. "That's one of the reasons we keep away from the commercial aspect of gardening. There's lots of reasons why we have the raised beds and individual plots. Being able to reach across a bed is very important if you're in a wheelchair and so the height of the bed is important. It makes for easy maintenance if you can get all round the outside of the bed and it helps with the initial planting and preparation. The beds are also practical if you want to get out of your wheelchair and sit on a cushion to do the work.

"The square beds makes it easy to plant in straight lines as well because you've got lots of edges to follow and it helps with things like numeracy, counting out the seeds, and measuring because you've got four equal sides. Because you've got a line to follow it's easy to fill. It's something you can do at home ."

Clients are referred to Trunkwell Park by social services, who provide their funding. People who come have all manner of disabilities from learning difficulties and mental illness to physical disabilities, and can be stroke victims, road traffic accident victims, or visually impaired. The only criterion is that the client has an interest in gardening and even if they don't want to continue with horticulture the skills they have learnt are transferable.

"There are lots of ways HT can help," says Chris. "There is the social aspect of it, working with people, or working on your own if that's what you wish to do. We're very lucky here because of this beautiful site and where it is. Also there's a massive choice of work

Karen Edwards, who has been coming to Trunkwell as a client for three years, is now helping new clients. "I like everything about gardening – just being outside, pricking out, getting my hands dirty. It's lovely here in the summer. We have a flower show in June – the first year I was here I got two firsts and a third for flowers. We do handwork as well, pottery, basketwork and we make a card for every client at Christmas."

and lots of things you can be doing. We don't usually do the same things week after week, although in gardening there's always the repetitive part of it. You always get a buzz out of watching something grow. To think you've actually planted it and you've helped it grow is amazing.

"There's also the whole structure of gardening and how gardening works. There's so many ways it can help individuals, no matter what sort of illness you have, or if you have a learning disability. Someone who's had a stroke can come here and the very fact of using the limb that doesn't work very well for simple jobs like potting can help tremendously. It has been proved time after time."

There's a permanent staff of six, and more than twenty volunteers who come in on a regular basis. Two of the staff, Lisa Bate, the volunteer co-ordinator and Alison Coe, administrative assistant for the volunteer programme, are being funded by the Consortium for Opportunities for Volunteering for three years to run a volunteer programme on the garden project, which involves recruiting, training and supporting volunteers.

Working in the raised flowerbeds at Trunkwell Park

There are volunteers of all ages and some with special needs. "We also have a buddy system where a few of the volunteers who are not able to undertake volunteering on their own and need some extra support are set up with more able volunteers to work together on different gardening projects," said Lisa.

"Some volunteers are simply interested in gardening and come along to use the gardening facilities. Other volunteers work with

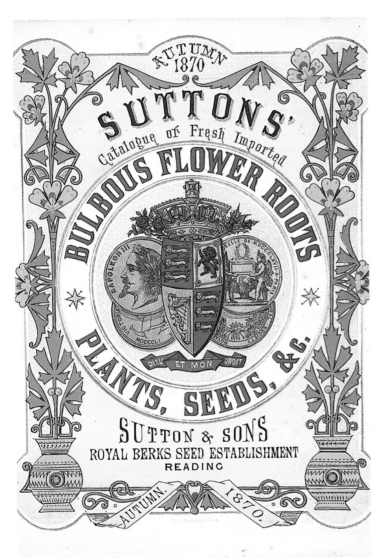

Above: Newtown
Community
garden in east
Reading. Story
on page 163.

Right: The
garden at Villa
Romani. Story
on page 167.

Above: The cover of the Sutton's root, plant and seed catalogue,
Autumn 1870. Story on page 137 Right: The Gothic Chapel at
Whiteknights by Hofland, 1819. Story on page 176.

The University of Reading campus at Whiteknights with fine trees screening Whiteknights (on the left) and the 'Lego' building. Story on page 179

Above right and below: The water garden recreated at Fernleigh House. Story on page 169.

clients, either in a group or one-to-one. Some volunteers carry out administration activities, not necessarily gardening. There's lots of scope here for people to come in and help with events, like the flower show and the open days, over the summer. We're very flexible so they can just turn up when they have a few hours to spare.

"Sometimes there's a fine line as to whether somebody should be coming along as a client or as a volunteer. For instance we have one gentleman who is visually impaired and his sight has started to get worse. He comes along here purely as a volunteer who enjoys gardening."

There is always new work to be done at Trunkwell as different parts of the site are developed. Sometimes people work with a client on a specific area of the garden, but generally everybody turns their hands to anything that's going on.

Alison said: "We always have an ongoing job list pinned up on the board so people know what jobs need doing as a priority in the garden. Chris goes around the site on Mondays with the two garden demonstrators and the land-use volunteer and they draw up the list for the next week or two."

Many of the volunteers are long-term unemployed who gain sufficient confidence and skills to get work. "They've come along here either through a government scheme or off their own bats because they want something just to get them out of the home," said Lisa. "And it really changes their personalities; they become more outgoing and confident."

Alison agreed. "A young chap came in who was painfully shy. He just wanted to come and work in the garden – he didn't want anything to do with the clients. He's been coming for seven or eight months and now he wants to work purely with the clients and training and the difference in him is incredible."

The fruit garden

The secret, they say, is the place itself. "There's a lovely relaxed atmosphere here and the gardens are beautiful," said Lisa. "There's so much to do and there's such a huge variety of people here. We've got all sorts and everybody can find somebody to pair up with or something to do which makes them feel comfortable. Nobody's under any pressure, which I think makes a big difference."

Anne Ibbetsen, who spends a day a week volunteering, feels it's the combination of the gardening and the people which makes Trunkwell so special. "Obviously I'm very interested in growing plants but the opportunity to work with people with special needs and combine an interest in gardening and people is fantastic. You get to know people through working with them, and perhaps learn more about them than if you just met them superficially.

"Of course you have to like gardening or you would just be miserable. For me the pleasure of gardening is seeing something develop, planting a seed and watching it grow, looking after it, seeing something flower or do what it's supposed to do. Just seeing it all come together in the garden."

That pleasure in gardening, in working together to achieve a high standard of work and good quality plants is something which everyone shares at Trunkwell whether they are staff, volunteers or clients.

Chris said: "Clients come straight in here to show me what they've done if they've planted something and made it look really good. They will try and show you, 'This is what I achieved' – and that's great. I remember one of the volunteers put a lot of brick edging around and he did it off his own bat. We give them quite a free hand in the general planning of the project on a day-to-day basis. That's good because nobody can come back and say 'I didn't like that' because they have all had some input into the project. I find that's the best way – to get lots of ideas, plan and agree it, and go ahead and do it. It's a democracy."

TROUBLE IN EDEN

... I am so taken up with pruning and gadening, quite a new sort of occupation to me. I have gather'd my Jargonels, but my Windsor Pears are backward. The former were of exquisite raciness. I do now sit under my own vine, and contemplate the growth of vegetable nature. I can now understand in what sense they speak of Father Adam. I recognise the paternity, while I watch my tulips.

I almost Fell with him, for the first day I turned a drunken gard'ner (as he let in the serpent) into my Eden, and he laid about him, lopping off some choice boughs, etc., which hung over from a neighbor's garden, and in his blind zeal laid waste a shade, which had sheltered their window from the gaze of passers by. The old gentlewoman (fury made her not handsome) could scarcely be reconciled by all my fine words. There was no buttering her parsnips. She talk'd of the Law. What a lapse to commit on the first day of my happy 'garden-state'.

Charles Lamb to Bernard Barton
September 2, 1823

u *for urban garden*

A garden for the community

The first spade went into the soil at the Newtown Community Garden on April 8, 1995, the date chosen for the day of action to start clearing a derelict piece of land behind the Eastgate pub. The land was originally the walled garden of a big house, older than the housing estate which had grown up around it. Once a Victorian kitchen garden, it had last been used for keeping pigs, and had deteriorated into a jungle of weeds, brambles and rubbish. From these unpromising beginnings, a garden was gradually created for the community.

The prime movers in the project were four horticulture students in their final year at the University of Reading, Jeremy Taylor, Ben Carter, Ian Hearn and Matthew Wells, who were all involved with environmental education. A meeting of Newtown Globe environmental action group fired their imagination and enthusiasm and they had decided to explore ways of improving open spaces.

"By March we had a list of sites we thought were potentially suitable for community gardens or new open spaces for Newtown, which is one of the most densely populated areas in Reading, and where we happened to live at the time," said Jeremy. "I think there must be well over 1,200 Victorian terraced houses built in the 1880s as housing for the workers at Huntley and Palmers and Sutton's."

The Newtown houses have small gardens, many of them north-facing, and either overgrown or concreted over. A community

Behind a pub in Cholmeley Road, Reading, one of the most densely populated areas of the town, is a community garden for the use of local people. It is a green spot in the heart of the town, complete with allotments, chickens, wildflowers and trees, where people dig their vegetables or gather for community events

garden with allotments where local people could grow their own vegetables seemed the most practical idea.

"We'd already noticed that there was this piece of land behind the Eastgate pub and when we came back to the Globe group in March we'd already approached Eamonn Munnelly, the landlord and he was keen on the idea," said Jeremy.

As the students talked over their ideas, the project began to take shape. They had to learn about the practical requirements of the project, raising money (they succeeded in gaining a BT environmental award), getting groups together, networking within the groups. Above all they had a lot of hard gardening to do.

"The spring growth hadn't really started when we first saw it," said Jeremy. "There were remnants of docks and brambles and a carpet of foliage, knitted with burnt-out television sets and odd bits of furniture, loads of masonry from the old Samaritans' building that used to be next door. Digging round there wasn't very nice – there was so much rubbish, relics of bonfires, broken glass and bits of nail, fittings from doors, bottle tops, screw tops, and a lot of tiles."

The first plan of action was bramble and debris clearance. "On the first day, we started gathering materials, like carpet, to suppress the weeds, and we got some hosepipes down," said Jeremy. "The biggest problems were bindweed, and the huge amount of water we needed. It's brilliant soil – probably imported because you need really good soil to grow a Victorian kitchen garden – but it doesn't hold water very well because it's so light. That's common for parts of Reading. It's perfect for carrots but not so good for things like spinach."

Posters were put up around Newtown begging tools, seeds, plants and bulbs. People were generous in their help. They were given tools, garden equipment and a van-load of wood chips for the paths. The community artist painted a mural (in anti-graffiti paint) on the fence and the project was on its way.

One of the big successes of the garden has been the allotment plots. The numbers have grown steadily and there are now 14 being worked by local people. In fact half the garden is now taken over by allotments, which is more than planned. "They are a good way of sharing gardening knowledge," said Jeremy. "On allotments you do chat to people and exchange information. People say, 'I've done it this way for years and it's never gone wrong.'"

There are still remnants of the old garden – the central pear tree, now decorated with chimes, the venerable walnut tree, which they believe is two or three hundred years old, and the pigsty, now used for compost. Landlord Eamonn Munnelly, who has enthusiastically supported the project, has now built a little livestock area near the pub with chickens and ducks. Plans for the rest of the garden include a wildflower meadow, an orchard area and a recreational lawn.

"I'd like to see the orchard come into fruition," said Jeremy, "I'd like to see a range of fruit on the south-facing wall, using the traditional varieties that were specific to the south of England. And it would be good to have a fig tree."

A community garden must suit as many needs as possible and regular social events are held there. In the summer of the first year, 50 or 60 people turned up for a barbecue and buffet. "All sorts of people brought food along and a guitar; old gardening folk wandered around the garden," said Jeremy. "It was the week of the local environmental art projects, and we had a green man made out of flowers in the garden. It was great."

The Eastgate pub has proved an ideal setting for the project, said Jeremy. "It's set off the road so though we're in a very urban area it's sheltered from the urban surroundings. It has got a water supply even though it's metered, it's got a community feeling, and it's totally secure. There are no problems with vandalism with Marty, the dog,

Jeremy Taylor surveys the Newtown community garden in Cholmeley Road, east Reading

next door, and a wall on the north and west sides. The entrance is always full of punters from the pub who often walk in and wander around."

The students who started the project have dispersed and left the area. Jeremy was away for a while but is now back living in Newtown. He still keeps a friendly eye on the garden but feels strongly there is a need for a long-term management plan with someone to co-ordinate and direct it.

"In the Newtown Community Garden project, we're trying to help people realise that it's just as viable to improve the environment in which you live as it is to improve the environment of the places you can escape to. Encouraging people to green their own gardens and have a say in the management of their urban space is ecologically interesting and biodiverse. They can help to improve the image of the whole community."

Jeremy also feels the project helped to raise the profile of students in Newtown. He remembers with delight in the early days of the project a regular at the Eastgate pub coming up to him and saying, "Jez, can I shake your hand. I don't like students but you guys have done something real good for the community and I'm really impressed. Good on you, mate, and I hope you do well in the rest of your career."

"When you get comments like that from people it's really worthwhile," said Jeremy.

SOUTHCOTE COMMUNITY GARDEN

"Why have a community garden?" I hear you ask. Southcote, south of Reading, is a 'green' estate with plenty of grass verges and open space, and everyone likes to see a bit of colour especially in drab corners. The story so far... When the plans were drawn up in 1996 for Southcote advice centre it was decided that the areas around it needed brightening up.

The council officials, along with representatives from the local residents' groups, drew up a planting scheme, with colour and form as prime considerations. The groups then approached anyone who could spare a plant or two, or time to help prepare the site.

As the area was rough grass, it was decided to enlist the help of professionals to clear it, which was done before 'plant day' much to the relief of everyone who was going to help us.

Then one Saturday morning, eager helpers, including children from the youth club and councillors, turned up armed with tools, keen to start. We dug flowerbeds, planted bulbs (donated by people), and various shrubs were given a new home, watched by a few inquisitive passers-by, until about lunchtime when we stopped for a break.

The garden is still intact, despite a few peoples' worries and it should mature into a nice spot to pass on your way to the local shops.

With a bit of luck most plants should survive the winter and next year we may increase the impact with annual bedding-plants, and yet more shrubs. Considering the negative opinions of a few, many of us think the garden has brightened up the area, something that never does any harm to anything.

John Bowsher

$\mathcal{V}$ for villa romani

The old gardener

It was a lovely warm and sunny day in the spring of 1956 and I was happily playing in the garden when I first came across 'the old gardener'. My parents had bought an old riverside house called Fortacre. The style of the house reminded my mother of her native Italy and it was decided that the name should be changed to her suggested Villa Romani. To my parents' amazement it was discovered that the house was originally called Villa Romani when it was built in 1896, and so the original name was restored.

We had all fallen in love with our new home and its charming garden where my brother and I played happily, with the added excitement of our discoveries including the old coins, white clay-pipes and stones that had obviously been tools in olden days.

It was in one of these happy moments that I found myself enveloped in a strong rather pleasant aroma of tobacco. Where was it coming from? I looked everywhere – nobody in sight!

A few weeks later I had exactly the same experience again. On the third occasion I decided to tell my father, who smiled and said, "Don't worry. It's only a gardener. Your mother and your grandmother and I have all had the same experience. Haven't you noticed all the old pipes we keep digging up?"

The neighbours had told my father that there had been an old gardener who was devoted to the garden and who loved to sit and smoke his pipe in the little summer-house that looked across the

Strange to think of a haunted garden yet DIANA NICHOLAS is convinced that there is a ghostly presence in the grounds of her beautiful riverside home, Villa Romani, in Maidenhead. This is no malign influence but a ghost drawn back from the other side by his love of gardens

grounds and the river to the Cliveden Woods. In the 1930s the grounds were split up and he was so upset that, sadly, he went across to the weir and ended his life. My father said he must love our happy moments in his garden and we must make him welcome.

And so it continued for more than forty years with perhaps one sighting. My friend had popped in with her little daughter, Sara, and we were sitting happily chatting in the garden. My father, then unable to walk without my aid, was indoors.

Suddenly Sara exclaimed, "Man in garden." Her mother and I both looked in vain but saw nobody.

But Sara pointed and persisted, "Man, mummy, man." So her mother told her that perhaps it was my father. Sara, who knew my father, just said, "No, mummy, no", and again pointed and said, "Man, mummy, man – there in garden". Could it have been the old gardener?

Haunted? The Villa Romani in Maidenhead

Few self-supported flow'rs endure the wind
Uninjur'd, but expect th' upholding aid
Of the smooth shaven prop, and, neatly tied,
Are wedded thus, like beauty to old age,
For int'rest sake, the living to the dead.
Some clothe the soil that feeds them, far diffus'd
And lowly creeping, modest and yet fair,
Like virtue, thriving most where little seen:
Some, more aspiring, catch the neighbour shrub
With clasping tendrils, and invest his branch,
Else unadorn'd, with many a gay festoon
And fragrant chaplet, recompensing well
The strength they borrow with the grace they lend.
All hate the rank society of weeds,
Noisome, and ever greedy to exhaust
Th' impoverish'd earth; an overbearing race,
That, like the multitude made faction-mad,
Disturb good order, and degrade true worth.
Oh, blest seclusion from a jarring world,
Which he, thus occupied, enjoys!

William Cowper
The Task – Book III
The Garden (648-676)

$\mathcal{W}$ *for water garden*

A garden of enchantment

Fernleigh House, a substantial Victorian property in Wokingham, appears somewhat an intruder sandwiched between much older terraced neighbours which date back to Tudor times. The house can be traced back to the late 19th century, occupying the site of three of the original cottages. For around twenty years from 1886 Fernleigh House was a private boarding and day school for 'young ladies… preparing for Oxford and Cambridge examinations'.

In 1911, already a tenant for many years at Fernleigh House, William Thomas Martin acquired the Anchor Inn next door from Brakspear's Brewery, later making common access on the first-floor landing. During the First World War the combined Fernleigh House served as a receiving hospital for the wounded. But at the end of the war, the pub succumbed to pressure from the Town Council to close its doors to the public because access to the stables in the rear garden was considered inadequate – horses had to go through the house! Since Wokingham at that time boasted one public house to every 99 residents (the lowest ratio in the country), and the pub had the Queen's Head to the left and the Hope and Anchor opposite, the regulars didn't have a leg to stand on – in a manner of speaking!

But William Martin was not seeking ale: he thirsted for land to feed his love of landscape gardening. He also acquired the Tudor cottage on his other flank. He now had a 100ft wide plot, to which he then added adjacent fields in 1928.

What have these in common? A set of fading hand-prints set into a bridge by erstwhile famous West End actors. A well-connected mayor with an interest in outdoor bathing. A rare local referendum forced by statute on an undemocratic Council. And lemonade. The answer to this conundrum is to be found at Fernleigh House, a Grade II listed building located near Wokingham's town centre and owned since 1988 by William and Pauline Tate. To be more precise, the answer lies in their intriguing Victorian water garden, as WILLIAM V TATE explains

Nowadays, visitors first encounter Fernleigh House's distinctive frontage. Its high spot is a large turret. The red bricks are covered with Virginia Creeper which turns scarlet in the autumn. But this creeper is no respecter of heritage: it rampages over leaded lights and ornately carved barge-boards, necessitating an annual trim. Nature always wins this uneven battle: scarred paintwork revealing onward-marching footprints, and bare wood cruelly exposed by the creeper's powerful suckers.

A handsome Victorian rose arch leads visitors into a secluded courtyard guarded by two pollarded lime trees. Long past their sell-by date, they stand sentry-like, struggling to maintain a dignified presence as their branches are whipped every Wednesday morning by the Morland lorry delivering beer barrels to the Queen's Head.

Overlooking this entrance is an elegant parapet surrounding a first-floor roof garden comprising a herb garden and vine-covered pergola. But we are more interested in what lies to the rear of the house, for much of which we have to thank William Martin.

So who was this William Martin, green-fingered benefactor of Wokingham? Martin was an enterprising butcher. Born in 1867 he ran away from school at the age of twelve, probably apprenticed to Richard Briginshaw and Son, local butcher. The son, John Warren Briginshaw, had acquired three adjacent plots on The Terrace in 1876 and built Fernleigh House, letting it to William Martin's elder brother Charles Henry Martin, Professor of Music and famous organist, whose wife became the school's principal.

By the age of sixteen William Martin had his own butcher's shop (telephone number: Wokingham 4), and soon ran a chain of seven shops in the Reading area. He first took up residency at Fernleigh House as a tenant of John Briginshaw in 1902, and was to buy the property from him ten years later.

Martin was also a political animal who rose to become Wokingham's Mayor by 1906 and held the office six times up until

A feature from the water garden today

1919. As a local philanthropist, he held a 30-year dream for Wokingham: an open-air swimming pool for the people. Yet in spite of his influence, he was frustrated by his elected colleagues, who refused to fund the project. So eventually, with a typical "if they won't build one, I will", he set to. With design help from his son Cathrow, head designer at Revilles, the Court dressmaker, he built a pool in his own back garden in 1932.

This was no amateur's construction: Martin's Pool won the national award for eleven years for the best outdoor pool in England. People travelled from miles around to admire the acres of landscaped gardens surrounding the pool and the rocky water garden, and to take tea. The delights were captured in a set of twelve postcards of the gardens, lovingly photographed by the famous society photographer, Gilbert Adams, one of Cathrow Martin's West End theatrical associates, who photographed the rich and famous – Sybil Thorndyke, John Gielgud, Elsa Lanchester, Nigel Playfair and Bernard Shaw, among others.

But the Pool's advertisement also heralded troubled times ahead: "Ample shelter from air raids or wet weather", it offered reassuringly. As it happened, the Pool had a good war. Originally camouflaged from enemy aircraft (it was on the flight path from the coast to Woodley airfield), the Pool was then commissioned to serve as entertainment to soldiers from the local garrison at Arborfield. Yet ironically the Pool was doomed to lose its final battle with the local council 50 years later. Councillors proved more deadly than the Axis powers.

Paradoxically, Martin himself sealed the Pool's fate, selling it and the surrounding gardens to the council in 1947, ten years before he

In the Pool's publicity material, customers were told "you can bathe in water pure as you drink. Stroll around the flower gardens, sit in deck chairs. Watch the bathers, fountains and water lilies. Sunbathe on the lawns and terraces. Children play in sand pit or bathe in the special children's pool. Morning coffee. Ices. Teas, confectionery and light refreshments. Milk shakes – all flavours. Visitors acclaim it a most delightful place".

The gardens of Martin's Pool

died, for around £8,000. Accused by his grandsons of "giving it away", he replied "I want them (the townspeople) to have something to enjoy forever". A hedge was planted to divide the site from the now private garden of Fernleigh House.

Fernleigh's principal pond is formal and classical, 55 ft long and set into lawn. In most years this is home to mating mallards, whose clutches of eggs and broods of ducklings are eagerly anticipated by the rapacious magpies gazing down from oak, beech and fir. The pond also serves as a regular port of call for herons and kingfishers, ever on the lookout for glistening carp, tench and bitterling catching the sun near the surface before the carpet of lilies (and blanketweed!) provides natural shelter through the summer months.

A second pond, 20 ft long, lies at the centre of a picturesque arrangement of cascading rock pools. Water starts and ends its journey here after being pumped into a small elevated reservoir hidden amongst a clump of trees.

Long-rusted pipes between the two ponds, under the lawn and from the houses, hint at an elaborate interlinked network supplying the whole water-garden complex, but forgotten for decades past. The roof garden once sported a fountain before being paved over, long predating the Tates' herb garden and pergola.

Restoration work on the sunken pond is relatively faithful to the original, but there are no diagrams showing the initial design. Indeed, there are some indications that the concept and the construction may have been flawed at the outset. Built on Berkshire sand, the pond's cracked concrete base was found to be very thin and unsupported when rediscovered in 1993. The pond had long since been filled in and had become so overgrown with compost and general rubbish that it took the current owners several years to realise there was a pond underneath. Bric-a-brac included the coloured garden lanterns used at the swimming pool's opening ceremony, suggesting its working life may have been relatively short.

In a May 1939 letter to the local newspaper headed "A Garden of Enchantment", a visitor wrote "... surrounded by rockery all ablaze with a profusion of coloured rock plants is a Lily Pond containing some of the finest specimens of water-lilies in the country. Gnomes cunningly hidden in the grottoes keep a watchful eye on enthusiastic sightseers. 'Glitterer' the green eyed cat gazes solemnly down from his elevated position in the trees. The splash of a waterfall is heard in the near distance and nearby lies a charming little representation of the old 'Willow Pattern' complete with weeping willow and bridge going over.... Everywhere is a riot of colour - aubretias, tulips, forget-me-nots, rhododendrons, sweet alyssum... Via winding avenues and wooded walks one comes upon a sunken garden, and here again is to be seen a lake in which Golden Carp sport themselves".

Similarly, the cascading pools had cracked and leaked and had been grassed over. Only the inability to dig down with a garden fork led to their rediscovery. The small reservoir was detectable from its outside wall, but it too had been filled in, had a tree growing in it, and had canted over and cracked under the pressure of tree roots.

Notable though the water features are, they probably impact the eye of visitors rather less than the sheer volume and variety of stone used to landscape the garden. It abounds with stone walls and rockeries, and the beautiful hart's-tongue fern. And there is a second ravine and another bridge. This too was overgrown. Again, it was some while before this ravine was discovered. A brick wall had been constructed under the bridge and the entrance was barred by a mass of wild blackberry plants, ivy and viburnum. At one end of the bridge, barring its entrance and disguising its presence, was a large sycamore tree stump, cut off crudely at waist height many years previously, but still alive and sprouting. Only after removing the gracefully arching roots across the span of the bridge was it apparent why they were shaped that way.

Fernleigh's lily pond in 1953

Most, if not all, of the stone was imported into the site, but some is not stone at all; it is pieces of an old kiln. Herein lies the clue to the lemonade part of our riddle. R White's reputedly had a bottle-making facility within a stone's throw, and there is also much cullet in the garden – coloured reject glass 'rocks', as well as numerous sea-shells and fossils. But no documentary evidence exists to support the bottle-making theory. There were, however, a number of local brickworks, and this appears a more likely source of fireclay. Whether for bricks or bottles, dozens of fragments of the kiln form one of the ravine's walls, still clearly stamped with the maker's name, B Gibbons Jnr Ltd, who manufactured fireclay and tunnel kilns near Stourbridge until his death in 1863.

But what of the referendum? As part of the reorganisation of local government in 1973 the Town Council (which continues to exist today) handed over ownership and responsibility for Martin's Pool to the newly-formed District Council for no charge. After almost 60 years as a public facility, the council later decided to realise its asset by selling the site to a builder for around £2m, arguing that in our climate the pool was only usable for about three months each year and it cost a lot to maintain. It sometimes made a small profit. But in 1989 – a good year with over 40,000 swimmers – it lost £94,000.

The public were outraged at news of the Pool's closure and sale, believing this showed scant respect for Martin's generous legacy. They feared loss of an attractive landscape garden, with a giant redwood and several large cedars, close to the town centre. By Act of Parliament, they forced a referendum upon the council in 1992 and won the argument handsomely, but the council was not obliged by law to act upon the result, and the residents' fears were soon realised. The writer witnessed the chainsaws toppling the redwood, which the builder had argued detracted from the site's viability.

Ironically, the Tates had earlier sought to have the council place preservation orders on the larger trees. But since the council both owned the site and also took the decisions on tree preservation orders to stop irresponsible people lopping them, they were told there was no need to worry! Furthermore the site was in a conservation area, which gave

But what, you might ask, has all this got to do with West End actors? Running between the ponds is a ravine, spanned by a stone bridge giving access to the lawn. It was into the concrete surface of this bridge which, rumour has it, William Martin invited some of his thespian friends to cement their fame for posterity. Coward, Gielgud, perhaps – we shall never know.

Fernleigh House today

automatic protection to the trees. The site – Poppy Place – now provides homes for 28 families.

The old market town of Wokingham is fast being engulfed by the commuter belt. Surrounded by light-industrial estates, warehouses and high-technology businesses, the town is not as rural as it used to be. But in spite of the housing development to the rear and the daily increasing traffic to the front, rock, water and wildlife combine to make Fernleigh House's Victorian garden an unexpected haven of peace hidden away from the bustle of the late twentieth century.

WEST READING'S TRAMLINE GARDENS

As a small boy I lived in West Reading and took some pleasure in the rather tinny-looking trams which ran up and down the Oxford road near my home. I travelled on them many times but this was usually when my mother went shopping in the town centre, so we nearly always got off at Broad Street. Thus by the age of six or seven the other end of the town remained somewhat mysterious as far as I was concerned.

At that time the return fare to the Wokingham Road terminus was one-and-a-half pence and, having raised this sum, I set off to ride on the open top of a tramcar to the end of the line.

The journey down Kings Road was particularly enjoyable passing over Crown Bridge (River Kennet) and Factory Bridge (the Canal, then usually known as The Cut).

Arriving at last at the terminus, I was pleased and surprised to find that the tramlines ended in a garden. It turned out to be the garden of a small café. I think the café must have derived much of its revenue from the tram crews. They worked very long hours under quite hard conditions. The trams had no windscreens and in wet weather the driver had to fix a tarpaulin to keep some of the rain off if the weather was bad. The tram crews would leave a large can to be filled with tea at the terminus café and collect it on completing the next journey.

At the Oxford Road end of the line the situation was rather different. The little green horse-trams of bygone years had terminated near Brock Barracks but the steady expansion of West Reading meant that by the time the electric trams came in 1903, the line ended near the Pond House, which had been built in the 1890s in what was then a semi-rural location. Not only was there actually a pond in those days but the public house had an 'arbour' where, in fair weather, customers could sit at tables under trees and consume their refreshments. The place still had a faintly rural atmosphere when I first knew it, but the rapid growth of Reading and the development of Tilehurst soon swamped the area with buildings.

Tony Barham

W for whiteknights

A garden surpassing all others

It is hard to imagine the glory that once was Whiteknights Park. Now a pleasant modern university campus, thronged with students from all over the world, it was in its heyday one of the most opulent gardens of the 18th century.

The man who created this extraordinary estate, and ruined himself in the process, was George Spencer Churchill, who was to inherit Blenheim Palace when he became the 5th Duke of Marlborough. In 1798 he moved his family to Whiteknights Park which had been owned by a Roman Catholic family, the Englefields, for the preceding 170 years. They sold up having finally given up the battle against 'the prejudices of the neighbouring gentry'.

The grounds were already known as a landscape garden of some repute in the 'natural style' made fashionable by 'Capability' Brown. In 1753 it was famous enough to have been visited by Horace Walpole who reported that "there is a pretty view of Reading seen under a rude arch, and the water is well disposed", although he was not impressed with the house (which was to be demolished in 1840).

As soon as George, the Marquis of Blandford, took over, he began ordering huge quantities of new plants as they arrived from Jamaica, America, and the Far East, where plant hunters were just beginning to penetrate – and the passion that was to help bankrupt him within 20 years took hold.

The 280 acres became an enchanted realm, described richly in

Whiteknights Park, now the campus of the University of Reading, was the inspiration for one of the most lavish gardens of its time. which became both the obsession and the downfall of a duke. ELINOR JONES tells the story

1819 in a book he commissioned from the author Barbara Hofland and her husband, a landscape painter. Entering through a three-arched gateway, the visitor would be confronted by an ancient ruined chapel, partly rebuilt in the fashionable 'Gothik' style displayed to advantage against a fine backdrop of mature trees planted by the Englefields .

Crossing a stone bridge over the lake, cleverly designed to appear like a river at this point, the visitor would approach the house and Botanic Gardens. A majestic cedar of Lebanon (which remains today) guarded this exotic fantasy world, which was entered through three oriental arches topped by crescents entwined in jasmine.

Among the delights within were a Chinese temple, covered with clematis, and a Japanese Garden. (The taste for all things oriental had been most spectacularly displayed in the Brighton Pavilion built for the Prince Regent between 1784 and 1787.)

The garden was divided into squares and circles, dominated by a large border of American plants. Velvety lawns were adorned with baskets of exotic and newly discovered delights such as begonias, and many rare trees and shrubs – including azaleas, rhododendrons and the first *Magnolia fraseri* ever imported.

The Marquis was so carried away in his enthusiasm for these never-before-seen wonders that he ordered seven greenhouses to be constructed, heated by the latest design of furnaces and flues.

Then came two aquatic houses, the Hothouse Aquarium, and the Greenhouse Aquarium, encrusted with beautiful rock, and latticed for creeping plants, containing a heated lead-lined cistern 26ft by 7ft. Just as outstanding was the conservatory 88ft by 20ft which, according

Who loves a garden loves a greenhouse too.
Unconscious of a less propitious clime,
There blooms exotic beauty, warm and snug.
While the winds whistle and the snows descend.
The spiry myrtle with unwith'ring leaf
Shines there, and flourishes. The golden boast
Of Portugal and western India there,
The ruddier orange, and the paler lime,
Peep through their polish'd foliage at the storm,
And seem to smile at what they need not fear.
Th' amomum there with intermingling flow'rs
And cherries hangs her twigs. Geranium boasts
Her crimson honours, and the spangled beau,
Ficoides, glitters bright the winter long.
All plants, of ev'ry leaf, that can endure
The winter's frown, if screen'd from his shrewd bite,
Live there and prosper.

William Cowper, The Task, Book III
The Garden (566-582)

to Mrs Hofland, was full of "the most rare and exquisitely beautiful exotics, displayed in jars, vases and bowls of scarce, costly and elegant china". A fountain, designed by an artistic aunt, was decorated with dolphins, lizards, fluorspar and Blue John, spiral shells and pink conches. Like her nephew, she gave free rein to her imagination.

On and on it went – a terrace garden, an orange grove, the Temple of Pomona, 'The Square' which displayed plants from China, Botany Bay and the Cape of Good Hope, the 1,200-ft long Laburnum Bower, and even a 'Striped Garden' containing variegated and striped plants. Most impressive of all was the huge magnolia wall, 20ft high and 140ft long, which was covered in *Magnolia grandiflora* – white flowers 10 or 12 ins across with a heady perfume.

Alas, such extravagances, matched in other areas of his life, could not long be sustained by his income, nor even by his inherited wealth, and in 1819 everything had to be auctioned off to pay his debts. George and his family went to live at Blenheim Palace, his family seat, but on drastically reduced means.

We are fortunate to have a permanent record of the park in those extraordinary days in the series of paintings made over two years by T C Hofland, although the artist was less fortunate. He was never recompensed for his work as his patron had by then exhausted his wealth. Unfortunately Hofland and his wife had had one hundred copies of the magnificent tome printed at their own expense, which nearly caused their own bankruptcy.

However, many of the trees and plants the Marquis had brought to Whiteknights lived long after his departure and in the 1840s the *Horticultural Journal* approved of plans to make it a national Botanic Garden to take the place of Kew and Chelsea which were suffering from the lack of space and the increased pollution of London. It pointed out: "… nor is there to be found in Europe a garden so capable of being made to surpass all others."

Of course, this never happened.

In 1849 Whiteknights was given to Sir Isaac Goldsmid, the first Jewish baronet (whose son built Park House, now the Senior Common Room) and it stayed in his family until the University of Reading took over tenure in 1947. In 1983 a plan to conserve the park was initiated, to renew mature exotics, clear scrub, and strengthen the lake banks and as this is carried out it is good to see the clear lines of the landscape reasserting themselves.

A place of mysteries

Much has already been written about the exotic gardens which once existed here in the days of the Marquis of Blandford. Little but the trees dating from that time is left now, but Whiteknights still has its own wonders, a place of mysteries and secret delights, and looks set to remain just as beautiful in its present, less formal style, far into the foreseeable future.

I first began my love affair with Whiteknights one snowy day over forty years ago, when I came, on a day trip from London, to visit my boyfriend (later my husband) who worked for the university and lived in lodgings in the town.

"I'll show you Whiteknights Park, where the university is going to have its new campus," he said. I had been charmed by the romantic looking cloisters of the London Road site, now Gyosei College, and thought that was exactly how a seat of learning ought to look. I was unprepared for the vast spaciousness of Whiteknights Park, as it was then known.

We took a bus to Pepper Lane; a country lane way out of town it appeared then, knee-deep in snow and winding more than it does now. When we entered the park it was under a grand archway at the end of a path – anyone ever wonder why Archway Cottage was so called? It spanned the road just beyond where the museum is now, by the hut which is used as the university mosque. It was a lovely, romantic archway; I wonder how many people still remember it? Further on, was a wall alongside the path, broken down in places. We scrambled through a gap on to a large, open space. The snow lay smooth, unbroken by footprints.

"There," said my boyfriend, "will be the university library, one day. I don't know if it will be built while I'm still working here." It was, and there it is now, huge and already with one extension and needing another.

BETTY O'ROURKE has watched the changes to Whiteknights over 40 years; seen buildings rise up in the park since the first university building in 1954. One of her pleasures is to take solitary walks there, but, after all this time, she is still discovering new places and new delights that Whiteknights has to offer

WHITEKNIGHTS.

When we wandered round Whiteknights Park that winter's day there were no university buildings, just a few beautiful old houses; Park House, now Senior Common Room, Whiteknights House, now Old Whiteknights House and used as a language laboratory, and Blandford Lodge, now hidden behind the College of Estate Management, popularly known as the Lego Building. The little gatehouse, Archway Cottage, looks much the same, but in those days was surrounded by a large garden, well-tended and full of flowers and vegetables.

The university had begun to build, however, and there was the skeleton of the Faculty of Letters, the first building to be erected in the park. Fifty years after acquiring the site, the university has dozens of buildings but has placed them mostly together in the centre of the park, leaving the majority of the 280 acres as a beautiful, unspoilt area to wander in.

A walk round the lake on a sunny summer morning is pure delight. The Canada geese and ducks abound and are friendly and unafraid, and for years there was a swan's nest near one of the bridges. If one is lucky, one may see the resident heron, standing so still on a branch overhanging the water that people might well mistake it for a model. But who knows the location of the old ice-house, now almost completely buried under the roots of a giant chestnut tree? In pre-freezer days, all great houses kept their food cool in summer by storing ice underground in these man-made caves. There was a time when it was still possible to enter the ice-house. Now, the tree roots have blocked the entrance.

And what was the original purpose of that strange pile of rocks at the head of the lake, where students hold picnics and light fires at graduation? For years, I thought it was the grotto, until I found the real grotto, further on, hidden inside a ring of bushes. Grottoes were popular in Victorian times and this one must have been impressive in

The 'grotto' at Whiteknights

its day. It's sad it has become so overgrown, the rocks fallen in over the years and young trees sprouting over them.

One can lose oneself in the Wilderness and imagine being deep in the countryside, miles from anywhere, until the path leads out to a university building, perhaps one of the wartime prefabricated 'Government buildings' erected at the Earley Gate end during the Second World War. Rumour has it the single storey huts were designed to be used as a hospital, and so have double doors which could swing open to accommodate wheeled beds or trolleys. As far as I can discover, the hospital idea never materialised, but there is a secret bunker in their midst which hints at mysterious, alternative seat-of-government plans. They are still used by the university for lecture rooms and laboratories, but are gradually being replaced.

There are intriguing mysteries to ponder over in the Wilderness. What were the concrete foundations, large enough for a small house, lying buried in the heart of the woods? There are tales of secret tunnels, nuclear bunkers for the post-war bomb era, but the only tunnels I ever found were part of a badgers' sett. We came one night to see them at play, but they did not appear that night.

I often wonder what new students think of their first sight of this, surely the loveliest university campus in the country. Those with long connections with the university will doubtless still have affection and some nostalgia for the London Road site, and there are still links with it. Not everything has yet transferred to Whiteknights, and the Great Hall is still used for degree ceremonies and examinations. The move to Whiteknights, though, was inspired. It has everything a modern university should have in a setting which has beauty and interest throughout the year from the vast drifts of daffodils in spring, to the myriad colours of autumn leaves, with summer's kaleidoscope in between. The planners of the park have successfully balanced the needs of the modern world whilst keeping so much of the area as a place for peaceful reflection.

What could be more glorious than the cedars in front of Senior Common Room? Great banks of rhododendrons make a colourful display in spring, but there is colour and interest all year round with the clever planting of so many attractive shrubs. The groundsmen do a fantastic job, with flowering shrubs surrounding the buildings and edging the paths leading from one to another. They plant interesting and rare trees, too, in the open spaces between the buildings.

X for xanthium

Notable by its absence

You are unlikely to find this in your garden. Be thankful. It's a weed. And it doesn't grow in Berkshire. So why include it in this book? The short answer is that it is the only plant in the British flora whose name begins with X, and we must complete the alphabet. A more positive answer would be that the book hasn't got anything about plants that are neither decorative nor useful, nor about adventitious plants; and it has only one other mention of weeds. What happens if you do find a Xanthium specimen in your garden? It provides a good example.

The fact that you are curious about an unfamiliar plant implies that you have enough knowledge to recognise its strangeness. You may even know how to use a botanical key, or you know somebody who can. You could track it down in Clive Stace's *New Flora of the British Isles* (2nd edition, 1997), which identifies the genus and species and tells you it is rare. If you then go on to consult H J M Bowen's *Flora of Berkshire* (1968) you will learn that it is very rare indeed to find it here.

You may perhaps consult your local museum, but one way or another, you with your plant specimen will finish up at the Herbarium in the University of Reading Department of Botany. It happens that the Recorder for the Botanical Society of Great Britain Vice-County 22 (old Berkshire) is located there. Your find will certainly excite interest since no specimen of Xanthium has been

DERMOT O'ROURKE finds the plant which conveniently fills the slot allotted to the 24th letter of the alphabet gives him the chance to explain how you track down an unusual specimen

reported in Berkshire since 1918.

How do we know? At the turn of the last century an Oxford botanist called George Claridge Druce examined and collected reports on the flora of this and neighbouring counties, and published the first comprehensive account, which includes only five sightings of Xanthium species. Then in the 1960s a systematic survey of the vice-county's flora was undertaken, and the results edited by Humphrey Bowen. Since then occasional reports have been noted by the Vice-County Recorder, but Xanthium has not been reported since Druce's day.

As the English name cocklebur implies, the distinguishing feature of this plant is its large bur. By the way, 'cockle' here comes from a Latin word for seed or grain, while Linnaeus's name derives from an ancient Greek plant called xanthion which provided a yellow dye. The cockleburs are probably native to South America, but have been widely distributed on the coats of animals. They have seeded in this country mostly from wool waste, and one might expect to have found them near woollen mills. Nowadays some species have been imported with grain seeds, occurring therefore in cornfields; with oil-seed, and found in rubbish dumps; and with birdseed. We have all heard of the cannabis plants appearing from the latter source; spiny cocklebur is likely to have the same origin, and is therefore the only one likely to turn up in the garden.

Don't worry. It's not a serious weed, here. It's a different matter in Australia where 'a plant growing in the wrong place' means anywhere near sheep.

Spiny Cocklebur (Xanthium spinosum)

Y for yew

Tree of death – and life

"The bow was made in England: of true wood, of yew-wood, the wood of English bows." Sir Arthur Conan Doyle was right, up to a point. What he didn't say was that the wood probably came from Spain, as it did throughout the Middle Ages.

The story of the yew tree, and of individual trees, is rife with speculation and myth. Of the two native British evergreen trees (counting juniper and box as shrubs), only yew was found in southern England. It grows on limestone and chalk. Native yew-woods are rare. None survived in Berkshire though we still find yew prevalent in some areas of the chalk notably around Aldworth. It happens that it is in the churchyard there that we find our best-known example of an ancient churchyard yew. Uprooted in a storm in January 1976, part of the trunk survives and still shows signs of life. Thankfully there are three other well-grown yews in the churchyard.

The yews commonly described as 'more than 1,000 years old', or as 'older than the church' may possibly date from earlier than the first Christian church on the site. Modern authorities believe that the yew was a symbol of immortality in the Old Religion, as the only large evergreen in the area. They suggest that some trees on sacred sites were protected, that the Christian church took over the sites and adapted the symbolism of the tree to the concept of eternal life.

A survey of churchyard yews by Vaughan Cornish was published in 1946. It arose from a questionnaire sent to English country parish

DERMOT O'ROURKE looks at some of the myths and legends surrounding that most mysterious of trees, the yew

The old yew trunk in Aldworth churchyard

clergy, but the response rate was not stated. Details of trees are patchy and usually only given for one notable tree or a pair. Cornish lists 15 Berkshire churchyards with yew trees; there were certainly at least three others (Cholsey, Hamstead Marshall and Ruscombe). Dates are usually speculative and not entirely reliable. The report from Yattendon of a tree with a 9 ft 6 in girth seems to derive from a written source rather than observation. One yew there, planted in 1666, took over 210 years to reach that girth, and it was finally uprooted in 1926. Its replacement, planted in 1893, can hardly have reached that size in little over 50 years. Again the tree at Waltham St Lawrence was planted in 1655. The 800-year-old yew ascribed to that parish is probably at White Waltham.

The poisonous nature of the berries, leaves and bark of the yew has given rise to the idea that they were planted in enclosed churchyards to protect cattle from them. This theory goes no way towards explaining why they were planted at all. Its Christian adoption might be linked with the use of another evergreen, the funeral cypress, in Italian graveyards and possibly fostered by Norman archbishops such as Lanfranc who came from Italy. While flowering branches of hazel or sallow were preferred for carrying in the Palm Sunday procession, it has been suggested that when Easter fell outside their flowering season yew branches were an alternative. All these are plausible.

What is not plausible is the preservation of churchyard yews for bow-making. Mediterranean yew has a closer grain than English yew as, strangely, has wood from more northern latitudes; and that makes a better bow. When Henry V needed a large supply of bows before Agincourt his bowyer was instructed to obtain yew staves from wherever he could, except church property. Clearly the churchyard yews were protected from this use because an archer's bow is made from the tree-trunk, using both sapwood and heartwood together to give it spring, the tree must be felled.

Yew is of course planted not only in churchyards but also as garden hedges or for topiary. Its poisonous nature must be remembered. Clippings may be burned, but they may also be sold. Yew Clippings Ltd, West Milton, near Bridport, buys them for export to Le Mans, where they are used to make a drug for treating some cancers. Yew may bring life as well as death.

**Old Yew, which graspest at the stones
That name the under-lying dead,
Thy fibres net the dreamless head,
Thy roots are wrapt about the bones.**

*Alfred, Lord Tennyson
from In Memoriam*

$\mathcal{Z}$ *for zymosis*

'Wine is also made with grapes!'

Every year, as autumn approaches, Italians all over Berkshire set aside a small space in their gardens and garages for the grand arrival. Wise old heads look up at the night sky and when the moon is in the right quarter, give the signal for the winemaking to begin.

The real diehards will have hired vans and collected their grapes themselves from cousins and uncles in Italy. Only in this way will they be able to choose their favourite blend of grapes.

The next level of enthusiasts will have been up since dawn, haggling with bemused traders at Heathrow's Western International Market, hoping to find the right quality at a good price. Still more will have bought their grapes from any local wholesaler able to deliver upwards of 30 boxes of wine grapes. All they can do is trust in luck and hope for a good batch. After all, this is serious business; not five-litre airing-cupboard amateurism, but 54-litre 'carboy' territory. And each family will make 300 litres or more. With so much at stake, nothing is left to chance.

As the new vintage gets under way in earnest, new technology and age-old traditions, new generations and old work together in harmony, just as they do back home.

The first stage involves crushing the grapes. Techniques vary from one family to the next, but most will start by picking over the grapes and throwing away any overly rotten bunches.

The best wine tends to be made from grapes that have been

Come late summer and you start hearing strange bumps and groans coming from your Italian neighbour's gardens; check the night sky before calling for help, advises LINDA MAESTRANZI, a 'Berkshire Italian' who has a personal interest in zymosis (fermentation). Better still, why not pop over and offer to help syphon last year's vintage. You'll soon learn that the fairies at the bottom of the garden start coming out after a litre – or two

removed from their stalks. There is a small, electrically powered machine that destalks and crushes at the same time, but most families destalk the grapes by hand and then crush them using a hand-powered mangle similar to the type used in making cider. A few families still swear by the old-fashioned barefoot method but most prefer to use the crusher.

The crushed grapes then fall into large, sterilised plastic drums where they are left to ferment (the zymosis part) for up to 10 days, depending on the weather. Where possible the drums will be kept inside as the temperature must be kept as level as possible. Too cold and the must will not ferment. Too hot and the wine will spoil. When the time is right (usually measured by a drop in sugar level but more often a gut feeling, especially for those whose families made wine back in Italy) the crushed grapes are pressed and the resulting juices transferred to large, 54-litre demijohns which also have to be kept at a steady temperature to continue fermenting. They are usually stored in the garage, or a brick-built garden shed with electric heating as back-up in cold weather, though one enterprising winemaker keeps his wine in a Second World War underground bomb shelter. (No points for guessing where he will be if the Four Minute Warning ever sounds!)

The must is left to ferment out before being carefully racked (syphoned) into a waiting demijohn. Tradition dictates that this should be done at the right lunar cycle, on a dry, still day. Superstitious maybe, but experience has shown that on wet, damp days the risk of infection from airborne spores is much greater. Racking is repeated as many times as necessary until the wine is clear, by which time it should, in theory at least, be ready to drink. However it's often drunk before reaching this stage and is the best cure for constipation I know!

The wine that isn't drunk straight away is left to mature until it is bottled, again only when the moon is in the right quarter. According

'Some say that if the moon is on the wane, the resulting wine will be fizzy but if the moon is waxing, the wine will be dull and lifeless. Then again others say the exact opposite. Watching my relations with differing views argue about the right time to do what is almost as much fun as watching the World Cup final – only without the sexy legs.'
Linda Maestranzi

Pressing the grapes in a Reading garden are Gianni Maestranzi (left) and Captain Frank Cadwallader

to more age-old tradition, the new wine should be drunk on November 11th, Saint Martin's day. In many parts of Italy *San Martino* is also the day when pigs are slaughtered and made into hams, sausages and salamis. The day ends with a Bacchanalian feast – the wine barrels are 'opened' and pork will definitely be on the menu.

There are several reasons why Italians in this country continue to make wine. Perhaps the main one is economic. Wine is an important part of every meal yet few would be happy to pay upwards of £3 a bottle – although if you were to add in the cost of all the equipment the saving is not as great as imagined. Then there is the cultural aspect. For many Italians, making their own wine is just like growing vegetables on an allotment. It has been done back home for generations, so why not continue to do it here in Berkshire?

And then comes quality. This can vary and depends as much on luck as on the skill of those involved. A good batch can surpass all but the most expensive commercial wines. I remember one year when the grapes came from Tuscany and were labelled as Sangiovese, one of the main grapes in Chianti. It was nectar-smooth, full-bodied and ruby-red. Because it was free from any chemicals, you could only get a hangover if you drank a whole demijohn! It left you feeling so mellow that one friend nicknamed it liquid marijuana.

The average 'vintage' is somewhere in between. The first sip can come as a shock to someone who has only ever drunk factory-made wine – it can be a little acidic – but the taste is very soon acquired especially if accompanied by food. The first grimace soon turns to a smile and "Another glass of vino, please". The best thing about it is that you can taste the grapes, which should please the TV wine critics who always seem surprised when they taste a grapey wine. Blackberries, peaches, plums, even coal, but rarely grapes. Perhaps there is some truth in the cynical Italian joke of the ailing commercial wine maker who said to his children as they gathered around his deathbed, "Wine is also made with grapes!"

"One year my father decided to rack the grapes on his own. He wasn't as scrupulously clean as he should have been and wine started turning into vinegar. That was the one and only year that we added Camden tablets to try and rescue it. It stopped the acetification but we still drank a lot of sangria that year!"
Linda Maestranzi

Vintage Berkshire